T0049564

Queer Villains of Myth and Legend

Queer Villains of Myth and Legend

A revelry of queer rogues and
outlaws through the ages

Dan Jones

RADAR

First published in Great Britain in 2024 by Radar,
an imprint of Octopus Publishing Group Ltd
Carmelite House
50 Victoria Embankment
London EC4Y 0DZ
www.octopusbooks.co.uk

An Hachette UK Company
www.hachette.co.uk

Distributed in the US by
Hachette Book Group
1290 Avenue of the Americas
4th and 5th Floors
New York, NY 10104

Distributed in Canada by
Canadian Manda Group
664 Annette St.
Toronto, Ontario, Canada M6S 2C8

ISBN 978-1-80419-135-4

A CIP catalogue record for this book is available from the British Library.

Printed and bound in Great Britain.

13 5 7 9 10 8 6 4 2

Publisher: Briony Gowlett
Editor: Scarlet Furness
Design Director: Mel Four
Illustrator: Jade Moore
Production Manager: Caroline Alberti

Typeset in 11/17pt Heldane Text by Jouve (UK), Milton Keynes

This FSC® label means that materials used for
the product have been responsibly sourced.

To all my delightful queer villains (you know who you are)

CONTENTS

INTRODUCTION

Come to the dark side.
We have the Babadook.

Underneath every hero's thrilling quest and every villain's delightful comeuppance there are archetypal narratives that power all our stories. With the magical ability to caution or inspire, empower or belittle, the timeless influence of the old tales should not be underestimated. That's why the pain of Circe is the same as that of *Buffy*'s Dark Willow, or the monstering of Medusa is like *Ginger Snaps*' grumpy teenage dropout reluctantly transforming into a hairy werewolf. These ancient ideas teach us many things; not least that heroes are straight and saintly, and that queer characters – those feminist witches, gay vampires, cursed monsters, horny demons and bulging goblin kings – exist only on the dark side.

Of course, many of us yearn to be just like the heroic, oiled-up champions and brave do-gooders of fantasy and mythology. But if you already sense you're something of an outsider, like so many future-queer kids do, sometimes it's the bad ones who fascinate. For me, it was David Bowie's Jareth dancing lithely across the gender boundary in *Labyrinth* – his impossibly tight leggings haunt me still. It was Medusa in the original 1980s *Clash of the Titans*, the cursed Gorgon sister slayed by Perseus, whose absence of backstory made me wonder, 'Just what has this woman done to deserve this?' And it was Lestat and Louis in the movie adaptation of Anne Rice's *Interview with the Vampire* and their immortal queer love, same-sex parenting and really, really great hair. These showstopping villains – complicated, clever and misunderstood – made the dark side seem, well, kind of fun.

And yet, these powerful mythic archetypes have often been used to push LGBTQ+ people down. We are more used to being the tragic, queer-coded villain than the glittering hero, and we've become vigilant about how we are portrayed. Watchful for those tired gay stereotypes, we roll our eyes at queer characters confined to punchlines or porny subplots, trans-identities used for plot twists, straight characters showing their depravity by having gay sex, all before we're bumped off at the end (they don't call the trope Bury Your Gays for nothing).

Valiant attempts to right this wrong have transformed culture, and, in recent decades, things have changed. Queer characters in art, literature, film and TV have truly evolved, but in the push for authenticity, something unexpected has happened. Although we have our own Hallmark movies, cute YA novels and mainstream Netflix mega-hits, something has been lost in our reworking of how queer people are portrayed. Have our aims of positive representation made our characters inanely saintly, bland and one-dimensional? Can't we be evil any more?

So many of our most enticing LGBTQ+ villains turn out to be mistreated in the narrative, or are marked out as evil *because* of their queerness. If we ignore their stories, we lose something of our own history and our sense of self. As we continue to lift up our champions, we shouldn't be afraid to get to know our villains, too. And so, these are the true queer villains of myth and legend, the age-old gods and goddesses, the fallen angels who have fallen in love, the lesbian vampires, bisexual ghosts and drag queen sea witches, and the contemporary LGBTQ+ Big Bads, on page or on screen, who are echoes of the ancient ones.

Meet the Minotaur, Medusa and Frankenstein's Monster, three misunderstood ancients trapped in their lairs, who offer us a queer perspective from their excluded positions. Volatile Hera uses her ancient powers of gender transformation, and Callisto, the victim-blamed nymph ravished by Zeus, is reimagined as as the powerful nemesis of Xena, the Warrior

Princess. Discover Amaterasu, the beautiful Shinto deity who switches off the sun (only to be lured back to the bright side by a sexy dancing goddess), and biblical villains from the much-maligned Lilith, Adam and Eve's witchy, problematic third, to Lucifer and his accidentally erotic statues commission by the Church, and Neil Gaiman's demon Crowley and his queer love for the angel Aziraphale.

Get to know Baphomet, the hideous horned pagan deity who fights anti-gay bigotry in modern-day America, and Mithras, the mysterious pre-Christian being who inspired hundreds of dark, men-only underground chambers across the Roman Empire. There are two complicated queer emperors, one of whom smothered his orgy guests to death with a cascade of flower petals and the other who built a sex shack on the Isle of Capri, and the Templar Knights and the court documents that suggest some brow-raising gay goings-on.

There is artist and filmmaker Derek Jarman's movie inspired by philandering bisexual painter Caravaggio and his devilish works, and all them witches, from Madeline Miller's Circe to Disney's Ursula from *The Little Mermaid*, and the Sanderson Sisters through to *Buffy*'s Dark Willow and *The Craft*'s Nancy Down.

Are all vampires gay? It certainly seems that way. From the bloodlust of Elizabeth Báthory, the world's most prolific serial killer of young women, to Carmilla, the lesbian literary vampire who predates Bram Stoker's Dracula (who, in turn, seems to be inspired by Oscar Wilde); Anne Rice's painfully embarrassing but loveable Lestat; Ana Lily Amirpour's chador-wearing skateboarding killer; and Tilda Swinton's Madame Blanc in Luca Guadagnino's reimagining of *Suspiria*. The 1970s and 1980s were glory days for minting new queer villains, from *A Nightmare on Elm Street 2*'s Freddy Krueger, to the riotous camp of Frank-N-Furter and bisexual Beetlejuice, *Doctor Who*'s the Master, and the bulging queerness of David Bowie in *Labyrinth*.

Just as we can be inspired by our heroes, there is also great wisdom and wiliness to be learned from our most mischievous and misunderstood queer villains. Come over to the dark side. We have the Babadook.

Some notes on the use of 'LGBTQ+' and 'queer' in *Queer Villains of Myth and Legend*

In this book, I use the term 'LGBTQ+'. It's an initialism in flux, with different communities and individuals using it in clever, creative and subjective ways. The + sign does a lot of heroic lifting: it encompasses a multitude of both fixed and shifting identities and intersections that don't fit neatly into lesbian, gay, bisexual or trans categories. Why? Well, I wanted to include everybody, from the ultra-masc Minotaur to gay gorgons, teenage werewolves and evil lesbian choreographers.

'Queer' is a catch-all for some, bringing together LGBTQ+ people into one sprawling family; for others, queer is an identity in itself. It's also an academic movement with a retro 1990s edge that seeks a new way of analysing a culture built around straight expectations, all to a Spice Girls soundtrack. Some might point out that queer was once a slur – and even though it is now widely thought to have been reclaimed, not all agree. What this shows, to me at least, is that both queer and LGBTQ+ are terms that imply huge diversity of thought and interpretation. And so, in these pages, queer relies on context. It will almost always be shorthand for 'gay' or 'lesbian' or 'trans', but it might sometimes point to something that, well, just isn't 'straight'. Oh, and one last thing: queer is a noun but also sometimes a verb. Confused? You'll get it, I know you will.

THE MINOTAUR

The bullish, big-horned lord of the (sex) maze

The Minotaur is the mythical half-muscleman, half-bull of ancient times, a flesh-eating horror who reigns over King Minos's labyrinth in Crete. Each year, gorgeous yet doomed Athenian 'tributes' are sent, *Hunger Games*-style, to their certain deaths until the Minotaur is slayed by our hero, Theseus. The Minotaur embodies unbridled sexual energy, the monster lurking inside the minds of all of us, representing our innermost desires. And to some, he is the perfect queer villain: a hung, strapping chimera, lord of the darkroom, stalker of the sex maze, who wants nothing more than the flesh of men in his mouth.

Alongside Ovid's *Metamorphoses*, countless frescoes, sculptures and mosaics, cups and bowls, the Minotaur has long haunted the dreams of queer artists. He clip-clops through Alison Bechdel's graphic novel *Fun Home* (2006) and hits the beach in surrealist poet Charles Henri Ford's impossibly racy short film *Johnny Minotaur* (1971), featuring Warren Sonbert and Allen Ginsberg, among others. And follow the thread from the original ancient epics to contemporary academic papers and you will find yourself in a labyrinth of self-published fever dreams. There's the eye-wateringly titled *Mated to the Minotaur* (2015) by Tate McKirk, *Lusty Labyrinth: A Minotaur/Human Gay Erotica* (2022) by Chris P Richards, and Delaney Rain's *The Minotaur's Mate* (2023).

In the Minotaurean legends, bulls and heifers play an outsized and unexpectedly sexualized role, and generations of the great King Minos's family are haunted by impossibly hench bovine creatures, with their bashful eyes and glistening, moist snouts. They nuzzle their way into King Minos's bloodline, with his mother Europa a descendent of Io, the nymph turned into a cow by Zeus to protect her identity from Hera. And, of course, there is Europa's own seduction by Zeus disguised as a bull.

But how did the Minotaur come to be? Poseidon, the great sea zaddy himself, became furious with King Minos for a small transgression and vowed to punish him. He bewitched King Minos's wife Pasiphae, causing her to fall hopelessly in love with her husband's prize bull. It was a cruel joke, but Pasiphae enlisted the help of Daedalus and Icarus to help her with a contraption so she could consummate her love – thankfully off-page. Soon, she gave birth to a baby Minotaur.

There is little written about the Minotaur's early days. King Minos was aghast at the newborn, punishing Daedalus and Icarus, but ultimately tried to accept his wife's new addition. As the child grew, his true nature began to develop, and Daedalus and Icarus were summoned back and made to build the labyrinth in which they would hide the Minotaur. Eventually, King Minos put his dark secret to use. When his oldest son was killed in the Athenian Games, he sought revenge by forcing the king of Athens to send seven men and seven women to Crete as a tribute – each to be devoured by the Minotaur.

In the Victoria and Albert Museum in London sits Antonio Canova's pale marble sculpture *Theseus and the Minotaur* (1781–83), and it has long drawn the eye of queer historians. They see a glimmer of gayness in the piece, not least Theseus's perfectly ripped body, the athletic locker-room repose and the slipping-off drapery exposing a flash of hero's bush. He sits heavily on the prone muscle-bound body of his conquest, his heaving buttocks on the creature's own crotch, whose bull-like head lolls back in the throes of death – or is it ecstasy? It is a favourite of Jack Shoulder, historian and co-author of *Museum Bums* (2023), who points out that many of Canova's confidants and contemporaries are thought of as queer, particularly fellow

artist Gavin Hamilton. 'Hamilton was involved at excavations at Hadrian's Villa in Tivoli,' writes Shoulder ('Uncovering LGBTQ Artefacts', Medium, 19 February 2021), 'and painted subjects like Achilles mourning Patroclus so he was well aware of LGBTQ themes from the ancient world.' Johann Joachim Wincklemann, the German art historian whose private letters show his adoration of nubile young men, and love of Michelangelo's perfectly honed Apollo Belvedere, also weighed in on Canova's project. 'We can surmise that this piece was informed at least by a queer gaze,' writes Shoulder, 'and that there is queer DNA in its making.'

If the maker isn't queer, then the inspiration might be. One hundred or so years later, George Frederick Watts – the British allegorical painter and sculptor – painted another Minotaur, only this time from a Victorian viewpoint. Watts's work feels like contemporary fantasy art, with glowing, dreamlike figures hanging out with angels or sniffing blooms. His painting *The Minotaur* (1885) has the monster gazing quietly out from a balcony in the sunlight, waiting for the next set of tributes to arrive, and is a study in quiet horror. For Watts, it's all about the body, as if the Minotaur's human essence is trying to climb out of its animal form. But what was monstrous to the Victorians now reads like the contemporary male beauty ideal. Watts's Minotaur is a hulk of triceps, lats and sinew, and pulled taut in a Greek-island selfie spot like so many shirtless fitness influencers posting from vacation: 'the struggle is real, guys'. It was painted in one delirious morning session after Watts had read about a new bill to both raise the age of consent but also further criminalize homosexuality, and he had his own desires to deal with – not least his impending first marriage when he was 46 and his wife was 16. Swept up in a very Victorian moral panic, Watts had the beast-like nature of man on his mind.

In all the stories and florid depictions, the Minotaur glows with queer energy. He is the unwanted son, rejected by society, with unnatural desires so frightening to the majority that he must be either tamed or destroyed. It is little wonder he is so fascinating to LGBTQ+ artists, some of whom imagine a different fate for the misunderstood monster: what might happen if the Minotaur stepped out of the labyrinth and into the light?

BAPHOMET

The Satanic Panic-inducing demon fighting anti-gay bigotry

Meet Baphomet, the goat-headed, human-bodied pagan deity who clip-clops his cloven hooves through centuries of ghost stories, horror movies and the feverish dreams of the conservative Christian right wing. With two fingers pointing up to the sky, and two more pointing down in a perpetual dad-on-the-dancefloor move, he's hairy, horny and queer as all hell.

Although the etymology of Baph is ancient, his earliest mentions as a deity are found in Inquisition transcripts dating back to the 1300s. There, he is linked to the Knights Templar, the mysterious Catholic military corps charged with protecting pilgrims. Their secretive ways drew suspicion and scorn and the fanatical soldiers soon found themselves accused of everything, from gay sex parties to worshipping a Satan-adjacent deity. Back then, Baph was a merely a rumour, a shadow on the overreach of the Church, but he soon entered the collective consciousness and became the antagonist of every scary story. He still has resonance with occultists and mystics, but some modern-day pagans point to Baph's neutrality. He isn't purely evil but embodies duality – good and bad – his pointing fingers symbolizing the phrase 'as above, so below'. He continues to haunt conspiracy theories of the Freemasons and the Illuminati, and powered the Satanic Panic of the 1980s. In recent years, Baphomet has become a cleverly deployed symbol challenging religious overreach and political hypocrisy and promoting pushes for queer liberation.

Enter the satanists, specifically The Satanic Temple (TST), a LGBTQ+ -friendly group for whom Baphomet has inspired divine-like fortitude. Co-founded by Lucien Greaves in 2013, TST uses symbolism like Baph to poke at those in privilege and power. Its superstitious imagery, incantations and berobed ceremonies hide an open secret: its members are nontheistic. They don't strictly worship Baphomet – or Satan for that matter – but exercise their right to do so. Born during the now defunct New Atheist movement, TST aims for the separation of church and state and is overwhelmingly liberal and queer-friendly. Its current focus? Upholding a woman's right to access abortion.

In 2013, TST infamously held its first Pink Mass over the grave of Catherine Johnson, the mother of late Westboro

Baptist Church leader Fred Phelps. Weeks after the Boston Marathon bombings, Phelps claimed that the Westboro Baptist Church would picket the funerals of the victims with its usual tiresome anti-gay messaging (graveside antagonisms were the Westboro Baptist's stock move in the mid-2000s). In response, The Satanic Temple held its very queer ritual. Lucien Greaves wore a headdress made of horns and two male couples and a female couple recited TST scripture, lit candles and kissed salaciously over the grave. TST claimed that the ritual had changed the sexuality of Catherine Johnson: 'The ritual was conceived to make Fred Phelps believe that The Satanic Temple had turned his mother gay in the afterlife,' writes TST at *TheSatanicTemple*.com, 'and succeeded in invoking the ire of the Westboro Baptists.'

A few years later, Baphomet was in the spotlight again. TST's impact litigation involves legal challenges to install Baphomet statues in public spaces where Christianity unfairly dominates, and in 2018 it found the perfect site. A Ten Commandments statue had been proudly unveiled on Arkansas State Capitol grounds, which, as TST pointed out, seemed to contravene the First Amendment that prohibits the government endorsing any particular religion. The satanists asked if they could install their beloved Baphomet statute there too. The answer from state officials? Hell, no. And so, Lucien and others drove an immense, 2.9m (7½ feet) bronze Baphomet statue, featuring the winged goat-man and two adorable children, 22 hours from Salem, Massachusetts to Little Rock, Arkansas to highlight their case against the state. This Baph already had something of a reputation. The statue had been crowdfunded and unveiled in Detroit in July 2015, with Lucien and TST asking for a simple donation for each ticket to the ceremony. Rather than cash, though, the TST had asked guests to sign over their soul – and, incredibly, 700 Baph-lovers were happy with the bargain.

Theatrical press stunts aside, there is something heartwarming about this modern love of Baphomet. In the US, where the separation of church and state is, at times, merely symbolic, those illiberal, conservative and anti-queer ideals can creep into everyday life. Lucky, then, that LGBTQ+ people who grew up hiding their identities in religious communities have found solace under the bat-like wings of Baphomet.

MEDUSA
The misunderstood monstrous femme

In a fire-lit death lair, Hollywood jock Harry Hamlin hides behind a pillar, his lithe muscle-twink body glistening, his soft curls giving top-3-percent TikTok hair-influencer energy, desperate to avoid being turned to stone. In contrast, his foe is so utterly hideous, so monstrous, that a mere glance into her eyes would mean certain death. But Harry – or rather, Perseus – has a plan. He takes the magical shield gifted to him by the gods and, using it as a mirror, tracks the slithering, reptilian humanoid through the shadows, his sword at the ready. The scene from 1981's classic fantasy movie *Clash of the Titans* shows Perseus, our hero, ultimately beheading Medusa, the mythic monstrous snake-haired femme that haunts the ancient tales. She is perhaps one of the best-known monsters of legend, inspiring countless sculptors, artists and writers from Dante to Shakespeare and Shelley, and even the fashion house Versace, all with different takes on her beastly form through to her transgressive beauty. But she is also the ultimate wronged woman, a survivor of abuse, feminist symbol and queer icon.

The earliest, most primitive depictions of Medusa have her as a lumpy, hand-made terror. In early depictions, the Gorgon was a grinning, hairy head with beard and tusks meant to protect its owner, though later on, Medusa, one of three Gorgon sisters, took on a beautiful, more human (although still terrifying) countenance. Medusa, the only mortal sister, then incurred the wrath of Athena due to her boastfulness about her ill-fated love affair with Poseidon – though more likely she was molested by the great sea god against her will in Athena's temple. This next aspect of the story is hard to square. Rather than punish Poseidon, Athena victim-blamed Medusa (if there are two things both the Ancient Greeks and Zeus's toxic pantheon loved, they are victim-blaming women and punishing those who boasted). To recap: the young Gorgon is violated by Poseidon, transformed by Athena into a vicious creature with snakes for hair and left to simmer and seethe until she is beheaded by Harry Hamlin. Surely Medusa wins the prize for the most wronged monster in existence?

Medusa has long attracted the attention of feminist academics and queer theorists who have deciphered her modern meaning and unpicked her supervillain status. Those early, bearded depictions on Medusa are of a female creature that refuses conventional femininity; she has a thoroughly queer body with the power to paralyse the jocks and chads of the heteronormative male world. Freud had some dark ideas about Medusa embodying the threat of castration, and in *Sexual Personae* (1990), Camille Paglia reminds us how the Gorgon's bloodlust is gender-specific, 'Men, never women, are turned to stone by gazing at Medusa.'

In her 2020 book *Warriors, Witches, Women*, Kate Hodges tells us that 'Medusa has become shorthand for a particular brand of strong female agency perceived as aggressive or "unladylike."' As Hodges points out, throughout history, outspoken women have been reimagined as the Gorgon in a bid to silence their voices and act as a warning to others who might step out of line. 'In the twentieth century, anti-suffragette postcards likened the protestors to the monster,' she writes; and 'during the 2016 American election campaign the image of Hillary Clinton's snake-bedecked raging head being cut off by her Republican rival Donald Trump – compared to Perseus – appeared on unofficial merchandise.' To Hodges, the message of these misogynistic Medusa memes is clear: 'Keep your mouth shut or we'll shut it for you.' Paglia seems to agree: 'Her hideous grimace is men's fear of the laughter of women.'

Back in the death lair, Medusa – a brilliant archer – picks off Harry's hunting friends one by one. Movie monster-maker Ray

Harryhausen has her clamouring on her hands, her snake-body twisting behind her like some hideous landlocked mermaid, determined to kill handsome Perseus. Eventually, our hero prevails and lops off her head, falling back to catch his breath, and Medusa has been vanquished. But the story of the Gorgon is far from over. Her bewitched head is a still-potent superweapon and Perseus uses it to defeat the Kraken. This symbol of Perseus the hero holding the Gorgon's severed head reverberates throughout culture, and its most famous depiction is Benvenuto Cellini's mid-1500s bronze *Perseus with the Head of Medusa*. With the Gorgon's head dripping with blood, it's a gory metallic masterpiece (Cellini had form here: he had slain his own brother's killer, who is thought to have acted in self-defence). The statue is in dialogue with the other nearby statues of the Piazza della Signoria in Florence, all of them marble, all of them men, as if Medusa has turned them all into stone.

HERA

Mount Olympus's master gender-switcher with revenge on her mind

For all his thrilling adventures, manly triumphs and problematic sexual conquests, Zeus has earned infinite fame, the world's most swole statues and a fanbase that fizzes with excitement every time he throws a thunderbolt. But there is a member of the Greek pantheon who would gladly see the great king of the gods cancelled. Zeus has his own personal antagonist, a divine, immortal sourpuss who is always there in the shadows, tutting and rolling her eyes. Many of the ancient stories cast Prometheus as Zeus's main enemy, the titanic fire-thief who helped the humans escape Olympian overreach, but it is his wife, Hera, who is the true villain of the piece. Or so the ancient stories would have you believe.

Hera is ancient – more so than Zeus himself – but her own mythology has become entwined and very nearly eclipsed by her younger male counterpart. She is the original goddess of women, and guardian of fertility, childhood and marriage, and was worshipped hundreds of years before Zeus strutted on the scene. She is even thought to be the first deity to have inspired the building of a closed-roof temple, in 800 BCE. Although a great beauty, Hera is always thought of as a curmudgeonly grump to Zeus's glittering handsomeness.

Hera's displeasure with Zeus supercharges many of the ancient tales. His endless attempts to nose under the togas of beautiful women and men eventually sees her drug him, tying him to his throne. He escapes and strings Hera up in the heavens as punishment. After being cut down, Hera agrees to behave, but she is too powerful. Although her dominance is permanently curtailed, she continues to enact revenge on Zeus's conquests and to flex her own muscles as Mount Olympus's master gender-switcher, casting spells of transformation on whomever she chooses.

Take Teiresias, the shepherd/priestess of two genders. The son of Everes the shepherd and Chariclo the nymph, the handsome young thing is hiking through the Peloponnese when he comes across two snakes getting it on. Disgusted, he hits them with a stick, after which a furious Hera punishes him by transforming him into a woman. But what is punishment to some is liberation to others and Teiresias loved her new form; she enjoyed several male lovers and became a priestess, hopelessly devoted to – you guessed it – Hera herself. Seven years passed before Teiresias saw another tangle of copulating snakes. Only this time she spared them, and Hera transformed her back into a man. Transformation is often a form of witchy punishment, from Hera's alteration of Teiresias to the witches of Roald Dahl who turn children into mice. But Teiresias experienced life from two genders – wasn't Hera's curse a gift?

Like all the best baddies, there is something incongruent in Hera's villainy. Sure, she poisons an island's water supply, killing hundreds to get to just one of Zeus's lovers, but she is also mistreated, ignored and thought of as a monstrous killjoy for thwarting her husband's most toxic urges. Hera experienced the same oppression suffered by ordinary Greek women in ancient times; their sexuality was shamed and concealed while men's desires were easily satisfied, whichever side of the bed they slept. Greek women were recognized by the state only upon marriage, and some argue that the stories of Zeus and Hera were propaganda for social stability – an honest rather than ideal union that might survive through the rockiest of times.

If all this seems too heteronormative for a truly queer villain, note that Hera is also thought of as the great tamer of man and beast. She is also a strategist; and in some stories, she merely pretends to play the part of the dutiful, faithful wife, while her real role is protecting her own power by controlling the excesses of her husband. She even borrows Aphrodite's girdle to seduce and therefore tame Zeus. And still, Hera is punished for her anger, her agency and her femaleness; and her power, older than that of Zeus, is feared rather than admired.

MITHRAS

The mysterious men-only S&M society of bull-slayers

Welcome to the underground cave-club of Mithras, a secretive society hidden in shadowy chambers beneath our oldest streets and buildings. Here were S&M hazing-like initiation rites, images of heroic male nudity, seven-course candlelit banquets and worship of a hyper-masculine, bull-slaying, pre-Christian deity. The first rule of Mithras Club is: you do not talk about Mithras Club. But the second rule seems to mark out its queer potential: entry to the Mithraeum, a sexy, dark, subterranean room, was exclusively for men only.

In the first century CE, the sprawling Roman Empire had an ever-changing line-up of deities, with Jupiter and Juno headlining Rome, Zeus and Hera overseeing Greece, and a hotchpotch of gods and goddesses in the Near East. Few had heard of Christianity, and at street level, men, women and children came together in their favourite deity's temples to perform sacrifices and group worship. But the cult of Mithras was different: male-only, hidden from public view and always congregating underground in a cave or carved-out basement. Evidence of these small, evocative spaces has been found across Europe and the UK, Israel and Syria – almost anywhere the Roman Empire had influence. Archaeologists have discovered Mithraic reliefs, sculptures and fancy facades depicting this fascinating god of machismo.

The Roman Mithras's origin story is primeval: born from a rock, he formed himself using his will, slayed a bull and then shared a banquet with the sun god before the pair enjoyed a ride in a chariot – all distinctly different images from the deity stories of its time. In some of the god's tiny temples, known as Mithraeum, he is depicted as a beefed-up naked man with a lion's head, entwined in serpents; but in every temple, there is a Mithras-slaying-a-bull relief or painting known as the Tauroctony. Mithras is often shown in a ray of light, in a cavern or cosmic egg-shaped space, surrounded by astrological symbols. The Tauroctony is always the centrepiece of the space, and it was an integral part of the cult's initiation ceremonies that evidence shows were brutal and cruel, with new recruits blindfolded, humiliated and threatened, and in which animals were sacrificed. These were true ordeals dealt out by chapter leaders known as paters and priests known as ravens, and they all ended with a ceremonial handshake.

Apart from around a thousand inscriptions of male names from Mithras-lovers themselves (soldiers, bureaucrats and civil servants), evidence of candlelit degustation menus and the hazing-like initiation rites, historians, archaeologists and other academics find it impossible to agree on exactly what the Mithras Mysteries were about. With its members sworn to secrecy, there is next to nothing written down and so the information gap tends to draw in some wild theories.

Roman military historian Michael Speidel claimed that Mithras is a version of Greek god Orion and that the astrological star-studded chambers presented the Greeks' knowledge of astronomy. Some claim that Mithras and Jesus follow the same saviour-god idea, with both cults having sprung up around the same time. Others point out that the bull-slaying god was just the Romanized version of Mitra, the Indo-Iranian god dating back to 2000 BCE.

With the Mithras Mysteries so, well, mysterious, the phenomena of these ancient, secret men's spaces evoke the more contemporary but just as hidden gay male spaces of the last few centuries, particularly the cottages and beats used by gay men before (and after) homosexuality was decriminalized. In modern-day European and UK cities built upon age-old Roman sites, those infamous public bathrooms and late-night clothing-optional basement bars, laser-lit dancefloors and steamy bathhouses all share the exact same subterranean landscape as time-worn Mithras temples. These are hazy, liminal spaces where the rules of everyday life are suspended and, for a moment, inhabitants can transform into something or someone else. All of them are covert worlds where men meet in secret, worship masculinity and, together, take down the bull.

LILITH

Eden's chief troublemaker and Adam and Eve's problematic third

'She ate men, drank blood, caused nightmares, and barren lands; the classic demonic femme,' says academic Brennan Kettelle of the most notorious, queerest villain of them all. Speaking on video series *Rejected Religion* in 2021, she made the case for bringing this seemingly malevolent figure into the LGBTQ+ pantheon. And so, meet Lilith, your worst nightmare.

If there's one thing Lilith stans and haters agree on it is that she is both ancient and multitudinous. The idea of Lilith or a Lilith-type entity first appears in 3000 BCE Mesopotamian texts. She is a wind demon here, a ghost or spirit there, a dust sprite or even a succubus sucking the souls of men as they sleep. Over the aeons, she developed into a Babylonian child-killing hag, a monster and a goddess, an early vampiric archetype and an enemy of pregnant women. For a time, her male counterpart was Pazuzu, the winged demon (referenced in *The Exorcist* franchise), and she appeared in the Greek pantheon as a lamia, a night-roaming demon who kills children and drinks blood. In the Book of Isaiah, a Lilith-like phantom hangs out with jackals and wild cats (making her the world's first cat lady); women really can have it all.

The Alphabet of Ben Sira, a satirical work from the Middle Ages, is full of tall tales and fart jokes. It is the first text to weave all Lilith lore together to make her one single entity and controversially places her in the Garden of Eden as Adam's first and somewhat forgotten wife. In *The Alphabet*, Lilith suggests she is equal to Adam, having both been created from the Earth. But this does not go down well, not at all. Soon, Lilith runs off to the wilderness, has sex with demons (because, why not?) and refuses to come home. Eventually, Eve takes her place and angels are sent to bargain with Lilith, who promises to murder 100 of her own demonic children every day.

Although *The Alphabet* is clearly a comedy, not everyone got the joke. In fact, this is where Lilith is established 'as not only a . . . monstrous wild feminine figure but also the anti-mother,' says Kettelle. Because of what seems to be a discrepancy in the book of Genesis, Lilith also looms large in Jewish mythos, where she is something of a biblical taboo. From here on, Lilith – a demonic main character – was destined to fascinate and inspire. Freewheeling, sexually voracious and a

chief troublemaker, she became the poster girl for problematic, opinionated women – no wonder Lilith is loved by feminists, lesbians and queer-leaning people everywhere.

Lilith being both loved and feared, depictions of her flicker between horrific warning signs to erotic fan art, offbeat theatre to lusty fantasy TV shows. There she is, combing her impossibly glossy hair in a Rosetti painting, or inspiring queer-leaning feminist projects like the women's music festival Lilith Fair and the reproductive-rights group Daughters of Lilith. She has even earned a queen-like place in extreme metal, with bands like Cradle of Filth, Behemoth and Septicflesh all drawing on her for inspiration. In 1964, arthouse cinema darling Jean Seberg was nominated for a Golden Globe for her portrayal of a mental-institution patient who seduces her therapist (Warren Beatty) in Robert Rossen's *Lilith*. Versions of her also appear in HBO's *True Blood*, Netflix's *The Chilling Adventures of Sabrina* and *The Witcher*, and perhaps even in Bebe Neuwirth's iconic character Lilith Sternin in *Cheers*.

C S Lewis's Narnia books, themselves a Christian allegory, have their legendary antagonist the White Witch as a Lilith stand-in. In fact, the witch, Jadis, is directly descended from Lilith (on one side, and from giants on the other), and gains immortality by eating a silver apple inside a walled garden in Narnia, a story with a strong biblical aftertaste.

'It was what I perceived as Lilith's pseudo-queer involvement with the Genesis myth . . . that kind of initially sparked my interest in examining her through a queer lens,' says Kettelle. The biblical story of the first man and woman, innocent and apple-hungry in the Garden of Eden, is all-powerful. It's here that those ideas around patriarchy and heteronormativity throughout Western culture seem to spring – and they are almost impossible to evade. 'Enter Lilith,' says Kettelle, 'this chaotic third element who . . . queers this Genesis myth and the dynamic between Adam and Eve.' In this way, Lilith is certainly transgressive; she refuses to be bound by expectation and, well, wants to sleep with whomever she pleases (in her case, demons). Feminist readings of the ancient myths point out the misogyny evident in Lilith's narrative and see her more as an emancipatory figure.

Like all the best queer characters, Lilith has been troubling gender and sexuality from the beginning and Kettelle's theories do great work in pinning down who or what she is. A wind demon, feminist troublemaker, or simply a chaotic third: doesn't Lilith sound like someone you'd want to spend time with?

CIRCE

The feminist enchantress
who turns men into pigs

Homer calls her the 'dreadful goddess with lovely hair', which is clearly a descriptor meant to warn the reader not to be taken in by feminine wiles, but instead does the opposite. Circe is the fascinatingly problematic enchantress with the glossiest, most delectable 'do. She is that always-in-the-midst-of-a-drama, *too much* friend you still feel oddly compelled to hang out with. Plus, she can turn men into pigs – what's not to love?

For centuries, Circe has been fantasized about by men. In the 3rd century, Apollonius gave her glowing eyes that shot out rays of light, in reference to her father the sun god Helios, and ancient drinking cups depict her transforming men into animal-headed beasts. In 1885, artist John Collier gave her a shapely bare bottom in his painting *Circe*; and in 1892, artist John Waterhouse zeroed in on her jealous streak in *Circe Invidiosa*. In all versions of the ancient demigod (her mother is the nymph Perse, making her semi-mortal), one thing is for sure: Circe is a total witch. Her knowledge of potions and magical herbs is immense, she is often depicted with a staff or magic wand, she sings like a siren, is jaw-droppingly beautiful and lives in a cabin in the woods. But how did Circe come to be ancient mythology's villain-with-the-great-hair, and what of her queerness?

Circe's early years seemed to be uneventful, especially compared with her family's infamous goings-on. As the overlooked daughter of Helios, she had to share the spotlight with her bisexual sister, Pasiphae, who scandalously charmed both Procris, an Athenian princess, and King Minos, he of Minotaur fame (see page 9). And Circe's niece, Medea, is a mythological celebrity and feminist icon. But Circe's time was yet to come. She is best known for her pivotal role in Homer's *Odyssey*. In a chapter when Odysseus and his men happen upon Circe's man-free island, Aiaia, the men are desperate, near to death, and, on seeing a column of smoke rising in the woods, they have no choice to investigate. There, they find Circe's dwelling, the iconic witch's cottage, and things do not go well – not at all. Circe serves the men wine and then bewitches them, turning them into pigs.

In almost all the ancient renditions of Circe, from the epic stories to art, she is villainous because she has broken an unbreakable rule: she has dominion over men, rather than allowing men to have dominion over her. Many of the Circe stories are warning tales; Homer is thought to have been writing about the woes of drunkenness (although being turned into a pig seems an unlikely punishment) as much as the nightmarish idea of a woman with power. Circe is almost always thought of as masculine and aggressive, gender nonconforming, forcing men into subservient roles, her animal houseboys.

In recent years, there has been much muttering about Circe in LGBTQ+ circles, largely down to the work of two female classicists. The University of Pennsylvania's Emily Wilson published a new English translation of *The Odyssey* in 2017 – the first ever by a woman – and in 2018 classics professor and author Madeline Miller, she of *The Song of Achilles* (2012) fame, published *Circe*, a novel reimagining the mythological main character's story. Miller's book sees her flesh out Circe's story by way of some clever changes and by exploring her origin story. Miller's Circe is no longer a great beauty and she falls for a mortal fisherman to whom she gives the gift of immortality – only for him to leave her for a prettier demigod. Furious, she misuses a spell and transforms a woman into a titanic monster, and is soon banished to her own island. It is here that she is visited – and is used and abused – by all manner of mythic men, until she is forced to use her magic again, transforming her attackers into swine.

Queer readers, their LGBTQ+ basements flooded by Miller's super-gay *The Song of Achilles*, feverishly read *Circe* on its release. Poised to enjoy something undoubtedly lesbian, they were, initially, disappointed. But what they found instead was a story of queerly feministic leanings – a retelling of the myth of an apparently evil temptress into one of female emancipation, revenge and survival, with a deliciously complicated main character. Circe's man-free island does seem to be something of a queer utopia, where she enjoys a life without gendered expectations. That is, until the men arrive.

Today, the misunderstood enchantress has her own DC and Marvel incarnations and her own Tarot deck, and Miller's bestselling *Circe* is a mainstay in airport bookstores. She even relents on her more problematic, villainous ways. Remember those human hogs that inhabit her island? They don't stay piggish for long. 'The truth is,' says Miller's Circe, disdainfully, 'men make terrible pigs.'

CALLISTO

Obsessive enemy of Xena, Warrior Princess

Meet Amazonian warrior Callisto, played by Hudson Leick, all teeth and tan, and giving blonde Nordic goddess vibes like a mythological-era Britney Spears. She's dangerous, remorseless and psychopathic, and her sole purpose in life is to destroy reformed hero Xena (Lucy Lawless) and everything she loves. She's obsessed. A casualty of Xena's warrior days, Callisto's parents were murdered when the Warrior Princess's army pillaged her village. Xena is guilt-ridden by the incident but Callisto is out for revenge and doesn't care who gets harmed in the process. The pair are bound by fate and, much to the annoyance of Xena's gal pal Gabrielle (Renee O'Connor) a queer energy pulls them together.

Callisto first appears in season one of *Xena: Warrior Princess* (1995), back when the show was arguably less queer-aware. Over six seasons, Lawless, O'Connor and creators Sam Raimi and Rob Tapert were increasingly conscious of their fandom's gay expectations. In the mid- to late 1990s, fans met in forums to share plot theories and their hopes for favourite characters, logging on via dial-up modems. Contemporary LGBTQ+ 'slash' or 'femslash' fan-fiction writers can trace their roots back to those early *Xena* boards, and it's here that the first glimmers of the show's LGBTQ+ themes were noted. Eventually, *Xena* secretly became the queerest, most transgressive, feminist fantasy TV show in the world, but it took time. And yet, as soon as she appears, Callisto – a terrifying and terrifyingly sexy villain – makes a surprising impact. If the relationship between Xena and her cute but vanilla Gabrielle was more a grower than a show-er, her sexual tension with Callisto feels instantaneous.

Every time Callisto and Xena meet, their will-they-won't-they energy dominates. Will Callisto satisfy her death wish? Will Xena have her swift retribution, or is there something else going on? Showdown after showdown, Callisto beckons Xena into dark, intimate, dry-ice-filled caverns, pacing around her like they're in a paso doble. Callisto is inside Xena's mind and, in the episode 'Intimate Stranger', she's inside her body, too. She tricks Xena into swapping souls and the pair spend a fascinating episode 'inside' each other.

In Ancient Greek mythology, Callisto is less a warmonger and more a nymph who pledges herself to Artemis by vowing to remain a virgin. Lolling around in the goddess's sacred skinny-dipping spot, she attracts the attention of Zeus. Soon, the problematic and extremely busy bisexual seduces Callisto by disguising himself as her mistress. The idea of the two women in a romantic tangle has attracted artists for centuries and depictions of the scene echo throughout the art of the 1700s.

'Callisto welcomes her mistress's passionate embrace,' writes Madeline Miller over at MadelineMiller.com, and 'for a moment it almost seems like we have stumbled upon a wonderful secret history.' Yet things are not so clear and the ancient world's Callisto is just as troubled and tragic as she is in Xena's. 'The audience knows better, because it isn't Artemis at all—it's Zeus,' explains Miller. 'The story gave its ancient readers just enough time to be intrigued, or titillated, or shocked [and] Callisto's error is played for laughs,' but Callisto's trust has been horribly abused.

'Call me humorless, but I'm not laughing,' writes Miller. 'Zeus reveals himself, rapes Callisto, then vanishes. The girl is doubly distraught – not only about the assault, but about the breaking of her oath of virginity to Artemis.' The goddess is furious that Callisto seemingly broke her oath, and Zeus's wife Hera is angry too. In the end, Zeus lifts Callisto to the heavens to protect her. In the ancient world, and perhaps the modern world as well, it doesn't matter if you did not consent; you're unlikely to see justice.

Back in Xena's world, her relationship with Callisto spans many seasons and her arch-nemesis's many forms, from mortal to goddess, demon to ghost. In the pair's final struggle, Callisto is transformed again, only this time into an angel. When Xena discovers she is pregnant (and is initially not happy about it, not one little bit), it is eventually revealed that Callisto, in one of the show's queerest narratives, had an angelic hand in it, having used her own divine spirit to impregnate her one-time enemy. It's confounding and confusing, and more than a little audacious, but Callisto nevertheless gives us something that, in 2000, truly broke boundaries. It's worth it just to see Gabrielle's face.

AMATERASU

The beautiful, brattish Shinto deity who switched off the sun

Amaterasu is the wonderfully brattish Shinto deity, an elemental supernatural entity from Japan's mythic age who governs the sun itself. Her power is near limitless, as is her potential to be dramatic and destructive; she is the Kardashian of ancient times.

Shinto, or 'way of the gods', is Japan's original folkloric belief system. It's a pathway through life, honouring the mysteries and magnificence of nature with rituals and rites, and – through its gods and goddesses – acknowledges a magical connection with the world around us. Much is made of the Shinto deities' fights, fury and falling in and out of love; as majestic and wise as each character may be, they live in a state of toxic excitement, enslaved to their own emotions, and Amaterasu is no exception. In the countless depictions of the sun goddess, via writings, paintings and ancient shrine art, she is beautiful, powerful, glowing with light and almost always swinging a sword to get her point across. This need to constantly self-assert feels a little queer to those in the know, and Amaterasu is often thought of as a bisexual or lesbian entity.

For instance, Amaterasu's origin story is deliciously queer. Her father, a creator deity called Izanagi, took a ritualistic bath to wash away the sadness after the death of his lover and gave birth to several deities in the process. From a tear in Izanagi's left eye, Amaterasu was born, the brightest deity the world had ever seen, with two more siblings plopping unexpectedly from Izanagi's other orifices. Amaterasu is close to her brother, Tsukuyomi, and between them they embody the sun and moon, respectively (when they are together, the sun and moon can be seen in the sky at the same time). Both have an uneasy relationship with the third sibling, Susanoo, who is always getting into trouble.

There are thrilling stories of Amaterasu in male battle dress, winning dominion over her most annoying brother with the flash of a sword, but the tale that best illustrates Amaterasu's accidental villainy, and her queerness, is the sun goddess's big moment: the legend of the cave and the mirror. After Susanoo's horseplay goes horribly wrong (Amaterasu's brother slaps a bloody skinned horse cadaver down onto her magical loom, killing one of her all-female gal-pal crew in the process), she finds herself sulking in a cave. Hiding away to perform an act of self-care might have seemed an essential step on Amaterasu's part, but her absence made the world plunge into a seemingly endless night.

Nothing could break Amaterasu out of her self-indulgence and, with life itself in peril, the gods knew that they had to do something: they appealed to the great goddess's sexuality. Enter the beautiful goddess of mirth, revelry, the arts and the dawn, Ame-no-Uzume. This minor deity, sometimes known as 'The Great Persuader' or 'Heavenly Alarming Female', danced seductively at the mouth of the cave and bared her breasts to lure out Amaterasu. Sure enough, Ame-no-Uzume's celestial orbs did the trick and the sun goddess soon peered out. A magical mirror hung in a tree reflected her own light, and she took yet another step out of the cave. Without missing a beat, Ame-no-Uzume rolled a rock towards the entrance of the cave, blocking it off, and Amaterasu and her life-giving light had returned!

Although the story of Amaterasu and her queer beginnings could have a positive effect on wider Shinto culture in Japan, there seems to be a long way to go. Before the Meiji era of 1868–1912, the old tales shimmered with LGBTQ+ characters, says queer Shinto priestess Olivia Bernkastel, pointing out the special emphasis on gay male relationships within Samurai

culture. But Western Victorian influences and attitudes changed all that, and 'as a result, a stigma began to rear its ugly head, and many important LGBT+ rights began to be lost,' writes Bernkastel in her article 'Shinto and LGBT+ culture: Connected from the ancient to modern era' (2018). 'Under pressure, openly gay and lesbian relationships; writings and art of them too – began to disappear.' But Bernkastel is part of a new, albeit ancient movement in modern Konkokyo (also known as Konkō, which means 'golden light') Shinto that formally announced its support of LGBTQ+ people in 2018, and has several queer clergy members, holds same-sex and same-gender weddings and shines as bright as the queer sun goddess who once hid her power from the world.

THE MAENADS

The raving *Yellowjackets* inspiration that will tear you apart

When the Beatles first arrived in New York in 1964, an official at Kennedy Airport 'shook his head and said, "We've never seen anything like this here before. Never. Not even for kings and queens."' *The New York Times* went on to describe how more than 3,000 young women had stormed the airport, desperate to catch a glimpse of the spindly all-male pop group from England. By the time the band got to Miami, there were 7,000 girls, leaving behind them a trail of destruction that included smashed windows and glass doors. 'There were girls, girls and more girls. Whistling girls. Screaming girls. Singing girls,' said the *NYT*, girls lost in the frenzy of pop fandom, a phenomenon that echoed across the decades, from the Beatles to the Backstreet Boys, Justin Bieber to Harry Styles.

The girls, whether they knew it or not, were taking part in an ancient, mythological female ritual. They were embodying the maenads, female worshippers of another pop god, Dionysus. Known as the 'raving ones', the maenads were famous for their booze- and drug-fuelled orgiastic pansexual revelries, for letting down their hair and letting loose in the woods. In the ancient texts, the maenads' ecstatic frenzy was realized through disinhibition, the suspension of morality, giving way to dance and movement, intoxication, queerness and sex – and, sometimes, murder. In the blur of bodies, hands transformed to talons and men (always men) were ripped to fleshy shreds. The maenads would dress in fawn skins and ivy crowns and waggle a phallic-looking thyrsus, a long stick swathed in vine leaves with a bulbous pine cone at the tip. Those 1960s girls squished up against the windows at JFK may have been without leaves and magical staffs, but they were no less maenadian – wasn't that glazed almost sexual grimace a little malevolent too?

Kaitlyn Tiffany in *The Atlantic* ('Why Fangirls Scream', 2022) says there is method in the screaming girls' madness and points out how the male gaze has influenced reporting on female fandom. 'Nearly all of the writing about the Beatles in mainstream American publications was done by established white male journalists,' she explains, pointing out that pop fandom has traditionally been seen as a part of feminine excess, and the opposite of masculinity. What could be less staid, strong and sceptical than the frenzied hysteria of the teenage girl? Tiffany – a self-confessed fangirl herself – underlines the overlooked intelligence of female fandom, the wry humour, creativity and community-building, and examines how any number of movements, from political activism to the Women's March, rely on the same powerful female group motivation.

In Victorian times, the maenads were the perfect villains for a society terribly afraid of sexuality. In the mid-1800s, the cultural prestige of learning Greek and studying the ancient ways meant that any number of impressionable young men and women were exposed to some hair-raising ideas. In one story, the maenads tear apart Dionysus's grumpy cousin, Pentheus, in the woods, and let his own mother – bewitched into thinking her son is a mountain lion – mutilate his body. In another, they rip Orpheus to shreds. Although sometimes the term maenad is used to describe a woman who refuses to worship Dionysus and is driven to madness as punishment, it is striking how little the apparent king of the maenads plays a part in their reveries. They may adore their male god but once the party has started and the wine is in full flow, he could be there or not. Soon, these screaming, murderous women played a political role, too, serving as a warning of what might happen if women were allowed to congregate, share ideas and organize.

In all the contemporary versions of the maenads, from C S Lewis's novel *Prince Caspian* (1951) to HBO's *True Blood* (2008), it is Showtime's rather queer *Yellowjackets* (2021) where the thoroughly modern maenad resides. The dual-timeline drama flips between the wilderness of a 1990s Canadian crash site of a high-school female soccer team (the *Lord of the Flies* part) and their present-day lives all grown up (the *Desperate Housewives* part). The flashbacks squelch with gore and gristle; there are blood pacts, horrific amputations, secrets spilled, and more than a little finger-banging in the bushes. The writers of *Yellowjackets* plumb the sticky depths of teenage female power, pushing the characters to the limit, removing societal expectations and watching on as they learn to let go (and indulge in a little cannibalism).

In fact, *Yellowjackets* is based, in part, on Greek mythology. There are knowing references to the maenads and their wine-loving Dionysian prince, and 'the series' very name and the name of the soccer team link the girls to the Greek god,' writes Sakhi Thirani in their essay 'Girls Gone Greek' (*JSTOR Daily*, 2023). 'Different from the flies invoked in the title of William Golding's novel, yellowjackets, like other wasps, are renowned for their love of wine grapes.' Thirani also points out that two of the characters – in something of a secret lesbian relationship – are allowed to take on a new, Dionysian form at a survivors' party in the woods, and thus have their queer love acknowledged. 'Taissa (played by Jasmin Savoy Brown), one of the team's stars, fashions two ornate leather masks so she and Van (Liv Hewson), her teammate and romantic interest, will match at the party . . .' writes Thirani. 'Masks are associated with Dionysus and his playfulness, and in *Yellowjackets* they play a vital role in facilitating this queer relationship.' Here, the destructive power of maenadism ends one way of living, and allows the building of another in its place, 'enabling each in her own way to deviate from normative society.'

Looking at the behaviours of Harry Styles's fans, or any contemporary pop diva, or even the feverish social and political queer activism of the young, perhaps we could say that there is something maenadic in many of us. One thing is for sure: in a straight, patriarchal world, there is clearly strength in numbers.

HARMODIUS AND ARISTOGEITON

The murderous male lovers
of Ancient Athens

Harmodius and Aristogeiton are the villainous murderers of an Ancient Athenian politician, brutally slain in front of a crowd at the Panathenaic Games. But they are also freedom fighters, ending tyranny and paving the way for democracy. Inspiring epic poems, heroic monuments and drinking songs, the pair has been celebrated for centuries. Behind the scenes, spurned advances, petty jealousies and vengeful humiliations make Harmodius and Aristogeiton's story read less like an emancipation narrative and more like the Real Housewives of Ancient Athens. But whichever of the great stories you read, one fact is clear: these two strapping young men were lovers.

When Peisistratus takes control of Athens in 561 BCE, he is a popular and just 'tyrant' (which once meant merely 'sole ruler'), earning him support from the poor and eye-rolls from elite Athenians whom he has knocked from their pedestal. But Peisistratus neglects to pass on his good nature to his sons and, when he dies in 528/527 BCE, his son Hippias takes his place, with his problematic party-boy brother Hipparchus lurking in the wings. The brothers soon sully their father's good reputation and abuse their powers, and Athens is uneasy. Enter local legends Harmodius, a handsome aristocrat, and Aristogeiton, his lower-class yet burly lover.

Hipparchus has a crush on Harmodius, but the object of his affection has eyes only for Aristogeiton and the tyrant's advances are rebuffed. This does not go down well and evil Hipparchus, used to having anything and anyone he wants, is aghast. Worse still, Harmodius tells Aristogeiton of Hipparchus's creepy come-ons, humiliating him. He vows to avenge his honour and sets about scheming a complicated bluff.

From a contemporary viewpoint, how the ancient texts approach the story of Harmodius and Aristogeiton is something of a wonder. The focus is as much on status and class, political power and murder as resistance as it is on the queer love story glowing at its core. The legend's delicious revenge plots and *Real Housewives* mic-drop moments truly delight, and nothing – not even man-on-man eroticism – is censored along the way. In fact, Harmodius and Aristogeiton's union is celebrated throughout culture, from the ancient writings of Thucydides, Herodotus and Aristotle to the works of gay British writers Edward Carpenter and E M Forster.

Back to evil Hipparchus's next move: to apparently smooth things over, he invites Harmodius's young sister to play an important and prestigious role at Athens's famous Bread Festival, but – in a plot worthy of a *RH* season finale – Hipparchus chases her away in front of the crowds, accusing her of not being a virgin (an essential aspect of the role). She is devastated, Harmodius and Aristogeiton are furious, and the pair make a snap decision that will ultimately see three men dead, the downfall of the house of Peisistratus and the birth of Athenian democracy.

Harmodius and Aristogeiton plan to assassinate both tyrannical brothers at the Panathenaic Games, but it doesn't go to plan. They stab Hipparchus but Hippias escapes, and young, beautiful, aristocratic Harmodius is slayed on the spot. Hipparchus dies and, later, Aristogeiton is tortured to death. In his remaining years, the surviving Hippias grows ever more despotic and is eventually overthrown three years later; but it is Harmodius and Aristogeiton, the gay murderers of his brother, who are remembered as the heroes of Athens.

Perhaps there was something politically convenient in thinking of Harmodius and Aristogeiton as heroes rather than villains? When Hippias was finally removed in 510 BCE, Athens found itself under new management. The Spartans took over and, uneasy about sharing the same fate as the unpopular ruler before them, they looked for ways to counter any potential resistance. They relied on Harmodius and Aristogeiton's star power, reigniting interest in the male lovers, who had the potential to become the Athenian's symbol of freedom and democracy. The Spartans quickly commissioned a public statue, and the fame of the pair grew. In the years after their deaths, they achieved near-immortal status, with commemorative coins, rousing drinking songs and a special law forbidding anyone to speak ill of the two men.

It was Greek historian Thucydides who, around a century later, found himself in thrall to the Harmodius and Aristogeiton's special connection, not just their pro-democratic street cred. He was entranced by Plato's notion of *eros*, the idea that love was the most powerful force that connects us, a sort of energy that powers political action, heroism and sexuality. Whether queer villains or heroes, Harmodius and Aristogeiton's *eros* has made them immortal.

ELAGABALUS

The murderous prankster of Ancient Rome

Meet Marcus Aurelias Antoninus, aka Elagabalus, the infamous teenage Roman emperor, part-time sexual psychopath and full-time prankster that historians would have us forget. His short, five-year reign (218–222 BCE) as head of the sprawling Roman Empire was fraught with scandal, political and cultural upheaval, an eye-watering hospitality and wardrobe bill and endless bisexual liaisons.

First, his nickname. Elagabalus is inspired by his family's elevated status as high priests of Syrian sun god Elagabal and young Gab's seemingly despotic attempts to impose the deity on the empire (much like queer king Akhenaten's failed reign in Ancient Egypt). In fact, it was Gab's family who secured his emperorship, powered by his grandmother, Julia Maesa, a once-exiled noblewoman who had the ambition and political nous to have the ruling emperor executed, installing her own family at the head of the empire, with her too-young,

14-year-old grandson as its leader. Would young, bisexual Gab have known about these machinations – and would he even have cared? What we do know is he was given the keys to the kingdom at his most hormonally fervent time and ruled not with his head, nor his heart, but rather what was under his bejewelled golden toga.

What came next was a freewheeling, devil-may-care reign of parties, pranks and terror; Gab and his hormones let loose. He took female and male lovers (the latter were more interesting to Gab if they be rich), dabbled in sex work, married again and again – once to a Vestal Virgin, an incredible social taboo that almost certainly meant the execution of his wife for breaking her vow of chastity. It was all in a day's work for Gab.

Ancient biographies claim that young Elagabalus played confidently with gender, refusing to conform to it. Cassius Dio, writing after Gab's death, is our main source on the emperor's gender identity, but some historians bite their lip at the idea of Dio being a reliable source. Over at Outhistory.org, Alexis Mijatovic uses Dio to officially claim Gab as transgender ('A Brief Biography of Elagabalus', 2012). Using she/her pronouns, Mijatovic writes of the young leader sensuously dancing for soldiers and of the rumour that Gab appointed ministers on the length of their appendage. Dio also claims that Gab consulted a physician to see if it might be possible to have a vagina, offering half the empire for whomever could do it, and married five women and a man (his burly chariot driver).

Gab introduced the first women into the senate (his mother and grandmother) and built his own at-home circus, hiding wild animals in his guests' rooms. Once, in Rome's Trastevere neighbourhood, he flooded a square with cheap red wine to re-enact a naval battle, and he even made the Roman Forum itself into an orgy venue. One prank was astoundingly creative and deliciously villainous. In the pages of the ancient *Historia Augusta*, the young emperor throws an incredible party and, at its climax, releases thousands of flower petals from a false ceiling. A painting, *The Roses of Heliogabalus* by Sir Lawrence Alma-Tadema (1888), depicts the scene beautifully, with an insouciant Gab lounging at a banquet table, bottom-up and swathed in golden silk, his orgiastic guests caught in a tsunami of rose petals, ecstasy and death. It is claimed that some of the partygoers died in the frenzy, drowning in the blooms.

There was no doubt: Gab was a problem. Eventually, in a *Game of Thrones*-style power struggle, again orchestrated by Gab's own grandmother, his inner circle was slaughtered, then his mother, and then himself. Once the murders were complete, then came the killing of the victims' reputations. Some suggest that Gab's truly incredible reign is too bad to be true, claiming Gab was a victim of *damnatio memoriae*, a Latin phrase that means 'condemnation of memory', a cruel revision of history once the victims were out of the way. The Ancient Romans always had an eye on their legacy and were the first to memory-hole their own salacious acts.

All this begs the question: is Gab's queer villainy merely post-mortem propaganda? Perhaps his juiciest stories are just homophobic, moralistic tales designed to elevate the status of his killers? These sticky legends, powered by queer sex and debauchery, have been Gab's narrative for centuries: James George Frazer, writer of iconic religion and myth study *The Golden Bough* (1890), called him 'the dainty priest of the sun [. . .] the most reprobate whoever sat upon a throne'. Greek historian Herodian (170–240 BCE) is thought to be our best top-tier source on Gab. His accounts of the past are evidenced and fairly well corroborated, and he too writes about a young emperor with a curious dress sense, tyrannical enforced worship, and about a young man who dropped his toga for anyone who caught his eye.

Despite the *damnatio memoriae*, Gab remains the most gossiped-about Ancient Roman emperor. There are few other ancient figures who have academics fizzing in excitement: Elagabalus is a queer mystery, wrapped in an enigma, draped in a golden robe – with at least one nipple scandalously in full view.

TIBERIUS

The Ancient Roman emperor who ruled from his Capri sex shack

No one expected Tiberius to be emperor. When Augustus died in 42 BCE, his three successors – men he had trained to be benevolent and powerful leaders and carry on his own legacy – all mysteriously died. Only Tiberius, Augustus's problematic stepson, was left: the definition of slim pickings. And yet, he found himself crowned as Augustus's successor. Tiberius ruled the empire for 22 years, overcame attacks, quelled unrest and pushed expansion, but he is perhaps best known for his secret hideaway on the isle of Capri: gender-bending bisexual love shack to some, depraved torture chamber to others.

Before he became emperor, Tiberius had his own path. He was a legal eagle, master strategist and military marvel leading Rome to victory in Germany and Armenia. But with Augustus's heirs all dead, Tiberius's emperorship was off to a wobbly start.

The senate refused to trust him and plots to oust him dogged his entire reign. Although a successful diplomat, he was unpopular with the Roman elite and eventually relocated to Capri, ruling from afar. And it was a villa here, perched upon a cliff on this sleepy island, that historians say was the sexual playground of the insatiable emperor.

Historians, especially those writing in the centuries directly following his death, detested Tiberius. Augustus was the GOAT and anyone who followed was not just a disappointment, but monstrous. But was this enclave of sexual oddities more an ancient Necker Island than some sort of Berghain-on-Sea? And what evidence is there of Tiberius's sex addiction? There is, it turns out, quite a bit.

Tourists still flock to the Villa Jovis each year, the emperor's one-time home, to see the evidence for themselves. 'Its bedrooms were furnished with the most salacious paintings and sculptures,' writes Suetonius, Tiberius's main troll, in his *The Lives of the Twelve Caesars* (1913 translation), 'as well as with an erotic library, in case a performer should need an illustration of what was required.' The 'performer' refers to Tiberius's guests, who might be called on to enact something depraved for the emperor's pleasure. 'On retiring to Capri,' says Suetonius, '[Tiberius] devised a pleasance for his secret orgies: teams of wantons of both sexes, selected as experts in deviant intercourse and dubbed analists, copulated before him in triple unions to excite his flagging passions.'

There's a lot going on in Suetonius's description of Tiberius's sun-drenched vacation home (not least the term 'analist'), and it is he who gives us the most stomach-churning versions of the emperor's time there. For all these theatrical depictions of Tiberius's home, though, there are other, simpler accounts. Cassius Dio, the historian who weighed in on the extraordinarily salty life of Emperor Elagabalus, spoke about Tiberius's love of wine being as great as his love of sexual experimentation, portraying both as bad as each other. Could the historians make up their minds: which emperor was the most depraved?

Tiberius's legacy might be forever overshadowed by his infamous Capri sex shack, but it has certainly given the island itself a certain notoriety. In Jamie James's *Pagan Light: Dreams of Freedom and Beauty in Capri* (2019), he charts the hedonistic artists, writers and bons vivant, problematic political thinkers, and revolutionaries who have been drawn to the island since Tiberius put it on the map. And wherever there are outcasts – elite or not – there are LGBTQ+ people. In the 1880s, Capri was a hotspot for men who loved men, and even Oscar Wilde and the young Lord Alfred 'Bosie' Douglas visited, further cementing the island's reputation for debauchery with the gay couple's devil-may-care queerness. To James, Capri has always been as much a refuge as a hedonistic gay party island: Wilde was recovering from his years in prison and wrote some of *The Ballad of Reading Gaol* (1898) there. Perhaps Tiberius's gift to Capri is not just toe-curling notoriety, but a place where the rules of everyday life are suspended.

ANNE BONNY

The tempestuous gender-nonconforming lesbian pirate of the Caribbean

Imagine Anne Bonny's delight in reaching Nassau in the Bahamas, more than 4,000 nautical miles and a world away from her birthplace in County Cork, Ireland in 1697. Then, Nassau and its British-controlled port of New Providence was something of an unofficial sanctuary for all who had sailed far beyond the eyes of the law – and none had drifted quite so far as Anne. If the legends are true, she quickly introduced herself to Nassau society by shooting off the ear of a drunken sailor who had the misfortune to block her path. No one stood in the way of Anne Bonny, the swashbuckling lesbian – or perhaps bisexual – feminist pirate.

Anne had long been known for her gender nonconformity and had dressed in some form of male clothing most of her life. In her early years, and in a bid to hide her existence from his wife, Bonny's father had taken Anne – his illegitimate

daughter – to London, dressed her as a boy and called him
Andy. But she was quickly discovered; Anne's father was cut off
from his wife's rich family and the pair soon found themselves
trying to make it rich across the seas in Charleston, South
Carolina. By 1710, Anne was a feisty 13-year-old with short red
hair, and would become embroiled in the saltiest portside
shenanigans. By 18, she was 'seen frequenting the taverns of the
port, on the arms of various buccaneers,' writes gay historian
Rictor Norton ('Lesbian Pirates: Anne Bonny and Mary Read',
14 June 2008), 'and there are stories that a would-be suitor was
hospitalized for a month after she beat him with a chair. She
once used her sword to publicly undress her fencing master,
button by button.'

Anne found herself in Nassau soon after her marriage to
small-time pirate James Bonny. She was promptly disinherited
by her now-successful father, but it was Bonny who helped
Anne escape the Charleston life and gave her what she really
wanted: the freedom of the open seas. In Nassau, the thrilling
hub of international piracy, she ditched James, enjoyed a brief
throuple with a Captain Jennings and Meg, his mistress, and
eventually ended up with celebrity pirate John Rackham, aka
Calico Jack, and another mysterious pirate, Mark Read. Mark
was one of Anne's great loves and was also known as Mary.
Mark apparently had a similar upbringing to Anne – born

female, raised as a boy to cheat sexist inheritance codes – and now had a somewhat fluid gender, drifting in and out of male and female jobs and roles. Together, Anne and Mark took control of two ships, cheated several male adversaries of their vessels, cargos and trust, and seemed to have the most incredible, queer-edged fun while they were at it.

'It has been suggested that Calico Jack may have come to New Providence as the paramour as well as quartermaster to a Captain Vane,' writes Norton, pointing out that Anne's closest pirate pals were unusually adept at plundering the booty. 'Another of Anne's menfriends was much more certainly gay. Pierre Bouspeut ran a coffee shop, hairdressing, and dress-making shop, for he was a designer of fine velvet and silk clothing.' According to Norton, Pierre heard that a French merchantman with valuable cargo would be sailing by and he and Anne posed as demonic otherworldly creatures to rob it. One night the pair doused a small boat, its sails and themselves with blood and approached the merchantman, which 'turned over the cargo of their vessel without a fight'.

Most of what we know of Anne and Mark is from Charles Johnson's 1724 book *A General History of the Pyrates*, itself the source of almost all pirate mythology. The book is a sacred pirate text powered by gossip, salacious stories and tenuous connection to fact. Seafaring folk tell the tallest, most

unbelievable stories, making the historical accuracy of Bonny's life hard to determine. She appears in Johnson's book, in wanted notices of the time and in other documentation in Charleston, Nassau and Jamaica, but the most exciting aspects of her life appear to be embellished versions of the truth. Eventually, Anne and Mark were captured and sentenced to death, both claiming they were pregnant to escape the noose. Sadly, Mark died in prison in 1724, but there is no clear record of Bonny's fate. Some claim that she passed away in Jamaica in 1733, while others say that she escaped to Charleston and died there in 1782, far older than her bisexual pirate adventures would ordinarily allow. Best to think of Anne Bonny forever on the high seas, the wind in her fiery red hair and queerness in her heart.

CARAVAGGIO

Derek Jarman's loud-mouthed, murderous queer painter

The work of British artist, filmmaker, writer and gay rights activist Derek Jarman (1942–94) is required knowledge for all queer people. His journal *Modern Nature* (1991) must be read, his music videos for the Sex Pistols, Marianne Faithfull and Patti Smith must be watched, and his films *Sebastiane* (1976) and *Jubilee* (1978) must be seen on the big screen at an obscure film festival. And if you haven't posted a selfie from Jarman's near-sacred beach hut and garden in the sad and stony wastelands of Dungeness, UK, are you even queer? Through his art, experimental film, theatre sets, activism and frank interviews, he was thought of as a 'radical maverick, an enfant terrible unafraid to rattle the establishment,' writes Alex Davidson for the BFI's website, in 'Where to begin with Derek Jarman' (2018). Jarman's work almost always included 'a loathing of any political and sexual oppression, a love for knowingly theatrical staging and tableaux,' and, as Davidson points out, 'a fascination with gay historical figures . . .' Which leads us to one of Jarman's best movies and most complicated subjects: his 1986 biopic of Italian Baroque painter Michelangelo Merisi da Caravaggio (1571–1610).

Jarman's *Caravaggio* is gorgeous, experimental, and yet one of his most popular and mainstream movies. It's also Tilda Swinton's first film, and a 'visually beautiful, sly and idiosyncratic biographical portrait of the great 17th-century Italian artist,' writes Glenn Kelly in *The New York Times* (2018), 'particularly interesting relative to contemporary discourse concerning artists behaving badly.' And Caravaggio did behave badly. In fact, the celebrated artist of *The Calling of Saint Matthew* (1600) was a tempestuous live wire, feral street-brawler and murderer – and rather queer with it. He was in and out of court (leaving behind more documentary evidence about his life than most of his contemporaries), menaced his landlady, beat up anyone who looked at him sideways, and fled Rome after killing Ranuccio Tomassoni after falling out over either a tennis match or perhaps jealousy over a shared lover. He then spent the rest of his days on the run, creating stunning religious art, in the hopes of a papal pardon.

The painter had a plethora of enemies, and accusing someone of being gay in Baroque Rome was a good way to get them into trouble. 'Caravaggio was almost certainly bisexual,' writes art historian and novelist Noah Charney in 'Caravaggio the Criminal' (*Salon*, 10 September 2017). Historians have traditionally disputed Caravaggio's queerness, finding the whole thing a little queasy, but Charney and many others claim that alongside his relationships with women (mostly sex workers), he was 'possibly also working as a young male courtesan in the service of several cardinals who enjoyed such company (and painting portraits of these consorts),' and probably enjoying a 'physical relationship with one of his models, Cecco da Caravaggio.'

And then there's the painter's work itself. He usually painted men and boys, and much has been written about his subjects' eroticization: parted lips, cheeky expressions, the curve of a wrist, and oh! the bare bums. Boys look suggestively at the viewer in both the painter's *Bacchino Malato* (1593–4, a stylized self-portrait), and *Boy with a Basket of Fruit* (1593). In Caravaggio's stunningly realistic *Amor Vincit Omnia* (1601–2), his naked little cupid – fleshy, and open-thighed – is uncomfortably thirsty. The piece shocked his contemporaries, some claiming that the model was a 'boy that laid with him,' and a rival, Baglione, created a retaliatory piece. His painting *Divine Love* (1602–3) mimics Caravaggio's but in Baglione's version, naked Cupid is in repose and about to bedevilled by a hulking demon, only an angel has stepped in to save him. What's more, Baglione gave the demon Caravaggio's face: it's the 17th-century version of a mean meme.

In Jarman's *Caravaggio*, the filmmaker doesn't shy away from the painter's bad-boy persona and throws in violence, hedonism and a seedy setting, and adds a little gay love interest into the plot. Played as an adult by Nigel Terry, Jarman's Caravaggio falls hard for Ranuccio (Sean Bean) and falls again into a tricky love triangle with Ranuccio's girlfriend, Lena (Tilda Swinton). 'There's a genuine, haunting power to Jarman's film,' writes Andrew Pulver in *The Guardian* (2005), 'which feels somehow like a [. . .] letter from a distant era – the pre-AIDS 1980s, when Jarman's high-minded camp seemed to be the future of art cinema.' Jarman was diagnosed with HIV in 1986, the year his *Caravaggio* was released. Perhaps he borrowed from the Baroque painter's tenacity, as he immediately went public with his illness, became a campaigner against the UK's anti-gay legislation, Clause 28, and soon addressed HIV and AIDS in his work, from his celebrated film *Blue* and the painting *Ataxia – Aids is Fun*, both displayed in 1993, the year before he died.

THE TEMPLAR KNIGHTS

The demon-worshipping gay finance bros and their (sword) swingers parties

As hallowed academics Drs Indiana Jones and Robert Langdon and their colleague Benjamin Franklin Gates will tell you, when it comes to the Knights Templar, half the job is working out what's fact and what's fan fiction. The enigmatic order, founded in 1119, has inspired countless fantastical imaginings, awarding its members magical powers, immortality, divine protection and the centre spot of every contemporary conspiracy theory going. But are they really the organizers of the most incredible gay party nights in centuries? Now *there's* a claim that's worth investigating.

First, a little history. Inspired by the First Crusade in 1099 and the occupation of Jerusalem (by murdering its Muslim and Jewish inhabitants), the Knights Templar, also known as the Templars, were originally a humble huddle of men known as the Poor Fellow-Soldiers of Christ and of the Temple of

Solomon. Their initial mission was to defend the Holy Sepulchre (Jesus's traditional burial site) and protect Christian pilgrims. But, over two centuries, the Templars shifted from protection to slick aggression; they were fighters in the later Crusades and officially recognized by the Catholic Church. Operating from a secretive *Avengers*-style superhero HQ on Jerusalem's Temple Mount, they answered only to the pope, and had huge political influence and incredible wealth (most Templars were finance bros rather than sword-swingers).

Almost 200 years later and the Templars, now a seemingly untouchable multinational megacorp, had a new frenemy. King Philip IV of France, in a regal version of 'she doesn't even go here', pointed out to the new pope Clement V, that the Templars had been lacking a clear mission for decades; what were they even for any more? The Church had already lost its foothold in the Holy Land, but Philip had form with the Templars and was hugely in debt to the order after hiring them for his own conquests. In 1307, King Philip ramped up the pressure and saw to it that the Templars, in France at least, were arrested and tried for all manner of things. That's where this queer mystery begins.

There had always been rumours about the Templars (are they, you know?), but in the trial depositions, every slight, put-down and lurid accusation was aired. The court heard confessions, extracted by torture, of sexy nude initiation ceremonies where rookie recruits would 'indecently kiss' Templar leaders, of gay orgy all-nighters and even of spitting on the cross. 'Philip himself was homosexual,' claims historian Rictor Norton ('4 Gay Heretics and Witches', 15 April 2002), 'but he stood to gain much wealth by outlawing the "heretics".' As the trial went on, the Templars were even accused of worshipping a mummified head and horned demon, Baphomet (see page 15): name it, and, according to Philip, they had done it.

'There is a great scholarly controversy over whether or not the Knights Templars actually were homosexual,' admits Rictor. 'Their initiation ceremony is well documented and has the ring of truth [. . .] it involved such things as stripping oneself naked, kissing the high priest or leader' – in all the wrong places, says Rictor – 'and engaging in homosexual group sex as a symbol of brotherhood.' This seems to be somewhat supported by the Chinon Parchment, discovered in 2001.

In the end, around 140 members of the Knights Templar, including Philip's nemesis, Jacques de Molay, Grand Master of the Order, were found guilty and burned to death. This untimely end for the Knights and their secrecy and the prosecutors' incredible claims have fuelled endless conspiracy theories ever since. Templars across Europe were retired, banished, or quickly shaved off their Templar-style beards and were shamed into hiding.

After 200 years in power, the Templars left behind a sizeable legacy, from religious relics to churches and other buildings (many European streets or neighbourhoods known as Temple have links to the Knights), and the Knights have inspired the Freemasons, temperance movements and a pop-culture legacy that has re-emerged in the *Indiana Jones* and *National Treasure* universes, Dan Brown's *The Da Vinci Code*, and video games like *Assassin's Creed*. One thing absent from these influential depictions of the Knights Templar are the gay sex parties, demon-worship, and cross-spitting. Perhaps we should remain sceptical about the Templar's spiciest stories until proven otherwise. In *The Last Crusade* (1989), on hearing yet another tall story about the Knights Templar, Indiana Jones rolls his eyes and says, 'I've heard this bedtime story before.'

ELIZABETH BÁTHORY

The blood-drinking countess and world's most prolific serial killer

Delphine Seyrig writhes across the screen in *Daughters of Darkness*, sinuous and sequin-scaled, an ageless 300-year-old vampiric legend come alive in the 1971 erotic arthouse horror. In an off-season vacation resort in Belgium (a horrifying prospect in itself), mired in a series of murders of young, beautiful women, newlyweds Stefan and Valerie encounter the glamorous Elizabeth Báthory and her young Goth-kid secretary. With her breathy tones, pencil-thin eyebrows and throbbing sexuality, Báthory wastes no time before she sinks her teeth into the beautiful but dull couple, subverting their tired heteronormativity and bewitching Valerie with her age-old lesbian magic. Oh, and there will be blood, and lots of it.

If *Daughters of Darkness* seems too fantastical to be true, it draws inspiration from historical fact. Meet the original Countess Elizabeth Báthory (1560–1610), lover of women and drinker of their blood, and the world's most prolific serial killer. Báthory's crimes were particularly gruesome, and the countess seemed to have countless kills up her frilled sleeve. With her servants as accomplices, Báthory is said to have tortured and murdered hundreds of women and girls over the decades in her relentless lust for blood. Her villainous reign ended after the death of her husband and the countess suddenly became vulnerable. A man chosen to be her protector became the chief investigator against her, collecting complaints from high-ranking ministers, gathering evidence and ultimately deciding on her fate.

Some historians claim that evidence against Báthory was scant; almost all of it was gossip, theory, or testimony via torture, and the charges amounted to a moral panic much like the infamous witch hunts of Salem, Massachusetts. There may also have been a financial motive to the gossip: debts owed to Báthory, of which there were many from high-profile men, were wiped out on her arrest. But others point to documents detailing almost 300 testimonies, some from young women claiming to be survivors, maimed and deformed at the hands of the countess and her servants. Either way, Báthory's noble status kept her from execution (although her servants each met a horrific demise), and she saw out her days under house arrest in one of her castles.

By the 18th and 19th centuries, Elizabeth Báthory's story had become a deliciously blood-soaked legend, and the idea of the female killer, a woman driven to the animalistic urges reserved for men, was rich for retelling. With its vampiric kills, crumbling castles and Hungarian location, the tale might be a precursor to the great classic vampire novels; and for many, Báthory's attraction to women – at least as victims – was bound up in her horrific acts.

In *Daughters of Darkness*, the countess seeks eternal youth, a theme also explored in Julie Delpy's 2009 Báthory biopic *The Countess*, which sees Delpy's character accidentally splashed with blood only to discover that it has magical anti-ageing properties. Delpy seems to draw a through-line to contemporary times, veering away from Báthory's sexuality and refocusing on how we are all brought low in our pursuit of ageless beauty. But *Daughters of Darkness* underlines the story's deliciously queer themes, from Báthory's erotic pursuit of Valerie and their heartstopping erotic kiss, to the countess's crimson nails and lips (*Daughters* is known as *Les Lèvres Rouges* or *The Red Lips* in France). Camille Paglia comes right out with it, naming Seyrig's countess an 'elegant lesbian vampire' in *Sexual Personae* (1990). The character Stefan, a sadist, is also queer: there is a reason he is so reluctant to introduce Valerie to 'mother', who is revealed in a phone-call scene to be a femme

man, and presumably Stefan's partner, in a 1970s horror mic-drop.

Queer viewers might roll their eyes at these problematic depictions of gay and lesbian characters in *Daughters*, with their immoral, sex-crazed ways, soft and seductive voices, gender nonconformity and great sense of style: they are a threat to the normal order of things. For Paglia, it is not as simple as the countess merely wanting to destroy heteronormativity; she wants to have a little fun while she does it. 'Evil has become world-weary, hierarchical glamour,' says Paglia. 'The theme is eroticized western power, the burden of history,' and with her ice-blond Marlene Dietrich hair and Third Reich colour palette, Seyrig's Báthory is coded as a fascist relic from WWII.

Daughters of Darkness is thought to be the movie that first successfully entwined sex and horror, changing the genre forever and ensuring that scary movies were overflowing with boobs and butt-cheeks for evermore; but it is also the perfect depiction of a queer villain, Countess Elizabeth Báthory. Delphine Seyrig's hypnotic performance toys with vampiric metaphor, the danger of queerness and the scariest trope of all: female sexuality, let loose.

QUEEN ANNE
The tempestuous monarch and her manipulated maidens

Queen Anne is the lumpen, emotionally frayed and forever ailing monarch who ruled as Queen of England, Scotland and Ireland from 1702, and later as Queen of Great Britain and Ireland, until her death in 1714. Her eyes perpetually watered, her gout incapacitated her and she was heaved about court on a sedan chair. Her legendary awkwardness gave way only to cruelty as she subjected her ladies-in-waiting to regal acts that went above and beyond, from forced humiliation to digital stimulation, or so the legend goes.

Historians (mainly male) have time only to roll their eyes at Anne's political legacy, pointing out her poor education and inability to make decisions. It is true that advisors would arm Anne with witty put-downs for official meetings with parliamentarians and noble-folk, but small talk was found to be near impossible; and Anne was known to simply pretend to talk, moving her lips with no sound coming out. Others point to her chronic shyness and her series of truly awful tragedies, including seventeen failed pregnancies with her husband, Prince George, and all but one of her surviving children dying before the age of two.

The source of Queen Anne's villainy, however – and her queerness – are the gossipy, mean-girl letters and journals of her apparent friend and confidante, Sarah Churchill. According to Churchill, interesting, attractive women soon became Anne's quarries, and the fickle monarch might just as easily ruin and banish them as she would look at them. Churchill is thought to have used this to her advantage, grifting her way upwards through Anne's court to ensure her own fame and fortune – and why not? Sarah is Anne's unofficial biographer, and her notes show her fascination – and disgust – with the queen. The feeling was not mutual – at first. Anne awarded Sarah several powerful, esoteric titles (Mistress of the Robes and Groom of the Stole, anyone?), gifting her extraordinary power and influence. Some historians talk of Churchill shadow-ruling the kingdom, acting as Anne's gatekeeper and quietly torturing her while she did so. Sarah writes that, in the hours following Prince George's death in 1708, Anne's love for her husband was surpassed only by her love of 'very large and hearty meals'. Eventually, Anne tired of Sarah's snipes.

Enter Abigail Masham, Sarah's young cousin, who was installed in Anne's bedchamber in 1704. She changed the queen's bandages, dressed her and fetched her bowl after bowl of steaming hot chocolate (Anne soon grew large due to her love of delectable things and incapacitation with gout). Soon, Abigail became Anne's favourite, their relationship hidden somewhat from Sarah until she discovered her cousin had enjoyed a number of special favours, including marriage to a houseman, witnessed by Anne herself, and a dowry (strictly, only Sarah could award such a thing, as Keeper of the Privy Purse). In turn, Abigail used her role to spy on the queen, feeding titbits to her favoured political party, the Tories. Sarah was in the opposing Whig faction and, sensing her power waning, got to work ruining Anne's reputation with salacious lesbian rumour. A popular poem at the time, probably authored or at least encouraged by Churchill, suggested that Anne was bedding one of her underlings: 'Her secretary she was not / Because she could not write / But had the conduct and the care / Of some dark deeds at night.'

The movie *The Favourite* (2018), director Yorgos Lanthimos's darkly comic version of Queen Anne's story, written by Deborah Davis and Tony McNamara, realizes a delicious lesbian love triangle between the monarch, played by Olivia Coleman, her class-hopping friend Sarah, played (with dominatrix fervour) by Rachel Weisz, and lowly cousin, Abigail, played by a wide-eyed Emma Stone.

There is a scene where Anne implores Abigail to pleasure her, resulting in an anecdote Olivia Coleman shared on a TV chat show with fellow guests Keira Knightley and Nicholas Hoult soon after the movie's release. 'Emma Stone was worried about me though because she had to finger me under the sheets,' said Coleman. 'In order to avoid finding anything you shouldn't have found [. . .] I asked the makeup department if they had a sponge [. . .]' Before filming the intimate scene, Coleman said to Stone, '"It's all right, there's a barrier, you'll be fine!"' Only Stone suddenly found herself digitally stimulating a large wet sponge. 'She was going up my leg and her face was a picture when she reached it! "It's all right, it's a sponge, it's a sponge!"' laughed Coleman.

CARMILLA

Before Bram Stoker: the world's first queer vampire

Sheridan Le Fanu's 1871 Gothic vampire novella *Carmilla* predates Bram Stoker's *Dracula* by 26 years and glowers with erotic queer power. Narrated by 18-year-old English woman Laura, the story takes the reader to the heights of horror via Victorian sexual repression, supernatural seduction and a lesbian love affair between Laura and beautiful stranger Carmilla, the story's chaotic top. Although the work was created within the bloodless moralism of the age, it feels surprisingly modern, has feminist qualities and is very, very queer.

After a carriage accident near the Austrian castle Laura shares with her widowed father, an odd turn of events brings Carmilla, a stranger, into their home to recuperate. At first, she seems like any other 18-year-old: she sleeps all day, snacks at night, avoids prayer time and has turbulent moods. But no one can resist the opportunity to remark how spellbindingly gorgeous this new girl is. Laura and Carmilla's friendship blossoms, but outside, a mysterious illness starts to claim the local young women; and soon Laura starts to feel a little drained herself.

Le Fanu may well be one of the forefathers of contemporary horror, but there are other themes in play here. The Irish novelist lived in an imperialist world, and that moral superiority and fragile sense of self in which the Victorians colonized the world haunts the text. There's a Gothic darkness out there, a fear of the unknown, and Laura's servant, Mademoiselle, is certainly thin-skinned. Her description of a Black woman, seen through a carriage window, stands out for its seemingly racist tropes. Otherwise, *Carmilla*'s feminist themes feel startlingly modern. There are no Victorian male saviours to rescue poor Laura from her fate, no handsome young jock to whisk her away; in fact, the men of *Carmilla* are mostly off-page, off doing something else. This is a story about women, and with Laura and Carmilla spending most of their time touching and caressing each other, Le Fanu has the pair lying together languorously in rumpled sheets. But this isn't an equal relationship, and through Laura's naive understanding of the world, Le Fanu obscures Carmilla's ultimate designs, hiding the implied eroticism in Laura's dreams. 'Sometimes there came a sensation as if a hand was drawn softly along my cheek and neck,' recalls Laura. 'Sometimes it was as if warm lips kissed me and longer and longer and more lovingly as they reached my throat, where the caress fixed itself.' It is hard not to read this scene as erotic, especially as Laura's dream is followed by an almost orgasmic conclusion: 'My heart beat faster, my breathing rose and fell rapidly and full drawn,' and there is a final, 'dreadful convulsion' – which is one way to put it.

Of course, Carmilla is not quite what she appears to be, with her otherworldly beauty, sharp tooth, odd sleeping arrangements (a coffin) and curious resemblance to a painting of an age-old noblewoman: she is a vampire. But Le Fanu's monster has a secret: she seems to be truly and tragically in love with Laura. 'With gloating eyes she drew me to her,' says Laura, 'and her hot lips travelled my cheeks in kisses; and she would whisper, almost in sobs, "you are mine, you shall be mine, you and I are one forever."' It makes the ending of the novella, where Carmilla gets her comeuppance according to vampire lore, all the more emotional.

And so was created the first lesbian vampire thriller, Le Fanu's own delicious subgenre, and there are many adaptations and reimaginings of this, the writer's most celebrated work. If Bram Stoker was able to draw on the scandalized life of his one-time friend Oscar Wilde to inform *Dracula*, he must also have borrowed liberally from *Carmilla*. Both stories have sleepwalking women, nibbled necks, first-person narratives and similar locations, and Le Fanu's vampire expert Baron Vordenberg could be a stand-in for Stoker's Van Helsing. Troubled *Carmilla* movie adaptations like Roger Vadim's *Blood and Roses* (1960) barely made it past the censors, and the enduring character haunts novels, comics and video games.

One of the most charming adaptations is the 2014–16 Canadian YouTube series, also called *Carmilla*, set in a girls' dorm room in a fictional Austrian international college. It's a single-fixed-camera affair, seemingly shot from an open laptop, with investigative journalism major Laura (Elise Bauman) complaining breathlessly into the camera about her annoying new roommate, Carmilla (Natasha Negovanlis). There's a missing girl, a mysterious dean and, when Laura steals Carmilla's Soy Tasty soy-milk carton, scrawled with the word 'mine', it seems to be full of – is that blood? There is trouble ahead, but also delightful queer romance, positive gender representation with a nonbinary main character, LaFontaine (played by K Alexander), and so much gay kissing. It is perhaps not quite what Le Fanu had imagined when writing in 1871, but the adaptation truly celebrates the novella's queer subtext and feminist qualities, and swaps its gory, stake-through-the-heart finale for a lesbian apartment-share in Toronto; Carmilla now has a happy ending.

KRAMPUS

The horned deity here to queer your holiday season

Let's wish Krampus, the horned-up and hairy demonic figure of Alpine yore, who loves to scare misbehaving children, a very merry Christmas. The devilish anti-Santa is the shadowy counterpart to Saint Nicholas and, every wintertime, the pair visit each household to enact their horrific reckoning. With Nick handing out oranges, walnuts and chocolate to the most angelic kids, Krampus slithers in quietly behind him, grinning in anticipation. He's hoping to meet a couple of bad ones, a bundle of birch rods ready in his hand. Malevolent and muscle-bound, covered in thick fur and wearing nothing but a tangle of chains, Krampus also has an impossibly long and pointed tongue: it was just a matter of time before he was absorbed into the queer pantheon of accidentally kink-adjacent deities, drag pageants, camp horror movies and gay erotica.

Krampus's origin story is as shadowy as the creature himself. He is certainly the dark star of Northern Europe's weird winter squad that includes the Slavic winter wizard Ded Moroz and the Yule Goat, but perhaps he has most in common with the monstrous Polish Turón or Balkan goblin Kallikantzaros. Paired with Bishop Saint Nicholas, they are all thought to have had a role in the ancient pagan winter celebrations held on 21 or 22 December, the winter solstice and longest night of the year.

Before the 1800s, Christmas was a ribald, booze-fuelled affair, and Krampus stole the spotlight. In Austria and Germany, Krampusnacht, aka Krampus night (traditionally held on 5 December), meant dressing up, getting drunk and running through the streets with gay abandon. Much like the American Santa Claus, he soon became commercialized: from 1890, he starred in a series of wildly popular Austrian and German postcards, each a comic-horror vignette with Krampus leering through each scene, chains in hand, his tongue waggling expectantly. In the early 1900s, Krampus got something of an upgrade: it wasn't just children he stole, but adults, too, and the cards themselves got rather spicy. In 2004, US art director Monte Beauchamp published a compilation of old Krampus cards, igniting contemporary interest in the character, who, along with the immigrants who exported his story was already present, lurking in the shadows, looking for more bad boys and girls in the States.

Then came 2015 and the dark comic-horror movie *Krampus*, its queer energy supercharged by the casting of LGBTQ+ favourite Toni Collette. 'Say what you will about Krampus,' writes Sadie Collins in their festive movie round-up for *Them* (29 November 2021), 'but he knows camp. Trapping a whole family inside a snow globe and terrorizing them in a mental simulation until they learn to love one another is a hilarious concept on its face, but it's also something every queer person has probably fantasized about doing to their own relatives upon traveling home, right?'

San Francisco's drag-nuns the Sisters of Perpetual Indulgence also understand the queer power of this transgressive entity and have been holding their annual Krampus pageant and fundraiser since 2018. Contestants show off their Krampus costumes, answer questions like: 'What is the perfect branch to spank someone with?' and perform for the prestigious Krampus crown (which, in 2021, was won by Menstrual Krampus, from Oakland). Krampus also features in author Quinn D'Angelo's *A Naughty Boy for Krampus* (2014) and L Eveland's *Kissed by the Krampus* (2022) where the protagonist, gruff army vet Chris Kringle, falls in lust with the ancient deity.

There's a freewheeling, anything-goes aspect to Krampus. With Saint Nicholas rewarding those who rigidly obey the rules, Krampus has always been for hedonists, the patron saint of those who want to misbehave. Of course, sometimes things go awry: in 2013, a boozy Krampus run in Matrei, East Tyrol, ended in near tragedy. Moments after the traditional garlic casserole was served, a brawl broke out between an estimated 200 Krampus and 'several hundred spectators' reported Helmut Mittermayr in *Tiroler Tageszeitung*, and one man ended up with a fractured skull. That year, Krampus season left almost 70 injured. Of course, Krampus isn't about the horrors of mob rule and garlic casserole, but he does inspire transgression, celebration and a little civil disobedience. Like the slogan 'Brav Sein' on the Krampus cards of old, we are expected to Be Good. But imagine what fun we'd have if we did the opposite.

DRACULA

The Oscar Wilde-inspired vampire king

Meet the original vampire king, an age-old undead monster and toothy Transylvanian, *charmant* nobleman and camp master of the dark arts. Those unfortunate enough to be drawn to his decaying castle are soon bewitched and befuddled, tortured with endless stories by the fire and eventually drained of their bodily fluids.

Drawn from folklore, or perhaps a real Wallachian prince named Vlad from the 15th century, and certainly Sheridan Le Fanu's novella *Carmilla* (see page 89), the character of Count Dracula is a weaving together of many ancient stories of nightmarish smooth-talking monsters. Author Bram Stoker's classic 1897 novel *Dracula* is considered the master tape of the vampire-king myth from which all contemporary depictions flow – from Bela Lugosi's *Dracula* (1931) to *Sesame Street*'s Count Von Count and even horror hostess Elvira, Mistress of the Dark. In the epistolary novel – a collection of diary entries and letters – handsome virgin and young lawyer Jonathan Harker leaves England for the count's mysterious Transylvanian castle to help prepare its owner for an international move. But things go bump in the night, Jonathan is seduced by the castle's other orgiastic guests, and Dracula himself is revealed to be a part-time bat and full-time vampire.

Dealing in unconscious desire, the loss of innocence, temptation and, ultimately, seduction and penetration regardless of gender, there is queerness screaming from the subtext. Stoker's novel is a genre-creating work of pure horror, and its florid depictions of the theatrical bachelor prince of darkness, of feared kisses and night-time shenanigans (is the count in love with Jonathan?) feel more than a little coded. It begs the question: just how gay is Dracula, and what of his creator?

Bram Stoker (1847–1912), the Irish writer, critic and actors' agent, is best understood through this vampiric bisexual, polyamorous outsider who will spirit himself into your bedroom at night and suck you dry. But another influence was Bram's relationship with hallowed gay author Oscar Wilde. Stoker and Wilde were distant friends, moving in the same elite circles, and had the same love of academia and the arts. In the polite societies of the Victorian era, same-sex friendships were treasured and queerness thrived secretly in plain sight. Of course, as Wilde found out, should LGBTQ+ love or desire ever openly speak its name then shame, social shunning and even prison awaited.

Bram was deeply submerged in academic, literary and theatre circles, so for him, queerness was all around. One of his contemporaries was fellow Trinity College Dublin scholar John Pentland Mahaffy, a giddy clergyman who published a discussion about Ancient Greek homosexuality, with Wilde's help, although he deleted the more salacious sections from further editions. There was a well-known cottage at the public bathrooms near Trinity on College Green and a male brothel close to Dublin Castle, where Bram's father once worked. Bram adored gay American writer Walt Whitman, and David J Skal notes Bram's delight in receiving a letter from his literary idol, a sweet reply to the fan letter Stoker had sent, remarking on Stoker's 'deep yearning for an ecstatic connection with another man' in his biography of the writer, *Something in the Blood* (2016). It was thought, at the time, that a woman might bring balance to the life of a man who preferred the company of other men, and literary historians write of a love triangle between Bram Stoker, Oscar Wilde and Florence Balcombe, who had once been Wilde's BFF and eventually became Stoker's wife.

There is a through-line from Stoker's vampiric subject matter to attitudes towards sex. Was he gay? Bisexual? And how should we account for 'his bottomless pansexual yearnings', as Skal so poetically puts it?

Wilde's conviction for gross indecency in 1895 was an atomic bomb of a scandal and Stoker found himself close to ground zero. As he lurched towards embarrassment and horror, his friendship with Wilde was instantly void, and it was in this atmosphere, just a few weeks later, that he began writing *Dracula*. The timing seems to be an integral factor: is Dracula – monstrous, perverse and larger than life – a version of Oscar Wilde? And is cute, innocent, twinky Jonathan Harker a stand-in for Bram himself? Skal sees Stoker as a sort of anti-Oscar Wilde, the antithesis of the foppish queer icon, and both a 'pair of Victorian bookends, shadow-mirrors in uneasy reciprocal orbits'. He even suggests that the vampire king's literary counterpart is Wilde's own creation Dorian Gray. It is impossible to know what Stoker truly thought of Wilde: in all his surviving notes and letters, there is no mention of his one-time friend. It appears that any such mentions were destroyed; the Victorian equivalent of deleting his number.

Many of *Dracula*'s characters are sexually voracious and the vampires' feeding frenzies are not-so-subtle depictions of sex. In the world of the novel, men are allowed to seduce other men, women have a confident sexuality (something of a shocking concept in Victorian times) and heteronormativity – although intact at the end – is given more than a fright. In the end, we can surely see Dracula – and perhaps Stoker – as queer: it's in the blood.

DORIAN GRAY

Oscar Wilde's murderous queer villain, uncensored

'It is quite true,' admits artist Basil Hallward, 'I have worshipped you with far more romance of feeling than a man should ever give to a friend.' The friend in question is Dorian Gray, the impossibly handsome, self-obsessed hedonist, muse to Basil, and murderer. 'Somehow I have never loved a woman . . .' continues Hallward, as if we hadn't already got the message. In Oscar Wilde's *The Picture of Dorian Gray* (1891), the love that usually dares not speak its name now shouts out its existence, loud and proud. These particular words were absent from the original novel, censored for their queer magic, and restored to the text only in 2011 on the thrilling publication of an uncensored version of this classic. Previously, no open declaration of love between men appeared on the book's pages (although, at the time of its publication, critics still found the book morally reprehensible), but that hardly mattered: iconic literary character Dorian Gray hardly had eyes for anyone but himself.

On a summer's day, Lord Henry Wotton observes Basil Hallward, an innocent young artist, painting a portrait of the very handsome Dorian Gray, our perfectly prickly antihero. Wotton – in love with the sound of his own voice – rattles on about the meaning of life, alighting on beauty as the most important ideal. In that moment, Dorian decides both to pursue beauty and to preserve his own, wishing passionately that his portrait – rather than he – might age and grow ugly. Soon he becomes the ultimate party boy, embarking on a kind of sexual rumspringa, trying (annoyingly off-page) every vice going. Apart from opium, the reader can only imagine what the young, attractive man experienced. Another restored line describes Dorian getting cruised in the street: 'A man with curious eyes had suddenly peered into his face, and then dogged him with stealthy footsteps, passing and repassing him many times.' Eventually, Dorian tries a spot of blackmail, driving others to suicide, and murders Hallward. His bewitched picture becomes more and more grotesque while he magically retains his own beauty – until he gets his comeuppance, obviously.

The characters are, of course, versions of Wilde himself. 'Basil Hallward is what I think I am,' wrote Wilde in a letter to his friend Ralph Payne. 'Lord Henry, what the world thinks me;

Dorian is what I would like to be – in other ages, perhaps.' At the time, Wilde was indeed like Basil, infatuated with his younger lover Lord Alfred Douglas, just like Hallward is obsessed with Dorian. Wilde was born into intellectual aristocracy and balanced his career as a celebrated literary figure with his own growing status as the source of lip-biting high-society gossip. In 1884, Wilde married Constance Lloyd and had two sons; but the more successful Wilde became, the less he bothered to hide his sexuality. He became part of the queer elite, scandalously started a friendship with openly gay art critic Robbie Ross, and by 1891 – the year *The Picture of Dorian Gray* was published – Wilde and Douglas were mired in an infamously steamy, barely secret affair.

In the tragic, queer-edged villain Dorian, Wilde seems to have predicted his own downfall. In the novel, Dorian is a man of privilege clamouring for beauty and pleasure at the expense of anyone and anything that stands in his way, until he finally goes too far. Four years after the novel's publication, Wilde's self-confidence seemed boundless, and he felt bold enough to take on the homophobic establishment, suing Douglas's influential father for libel after he publicly accused Wilde of being gay. Wilde lost everything: his reputation, his privacy (details of his sex life were revealed), his family and most of his queer social circle, who worried more about their own reputations than they did about the fate of their friend. His contemporary Bram Stoker was horrified at Wilde's fall from grace and wrote *Dracula* in the throes of the scandal, seemingly basing the character on Wilde himself (see page 101). Wilde was sentenced to two years' hard labour and then, after a misjudged trip to Capri with Douglas, ended up in Paris (where else?), physically and mentally broken. His writing descended into nihilism, and he died at the age of 46, destitute but with Robbie Ross by his side.

'From the moment I met you,' Hallward tells Dorian in the uncensored version of the novel, 'your personality had the most extraordinary influence over me.' It is hard to read these words without imagining them an echo of Wilde's own feelings towards Lord Alfred Douglas and the desperation he must have felt – just like Dorian – as his life came to an end. 'I adored you madly, extravagantly, absurdly,' he continues. 'I was jealous of everyone to whom you spoke. I wanted to have you all to myself. I was only happy when I was with you.'

FRANKENSTEIN'S MONSTER

The Frankenqueer outcast who just wants to be loved

Mary Shelley's groundbreaking science-fiction novel, *Frankenstein; or The Modern Prometheus* (1818), was inspired by a nightmare and penned when the author was just 19. She had spent the summer of 1816 with friends at Lake Geneva under endlessly rainy and grey skies due a volcanic ash cloud caused by the eruption of Mount Tomboro the previous year. Shelley hoped and hoped for inspiration to strike, and *Frankenstein* soon sparked into life. Presented in epistolary form as a collection of letters and journal entries, it slowly reveals, like a found-footage horror movie, its tragic tale, with romantic and Gothic elements, lots of untimely death, a snowy finale setting and a misunderstood villain at its heart. In the classic novel, heterodox scientist Victor Frankenstein embarks on a truly deranged experiment. Using stolen body parts and electricity, he attempts to create an artificial, intelligent, living being, but his success is his undoing and the scientist's ungodly 'Creature' is self-aware, hideous and hated by almost all who see him.

Shelley's characters have staying power. Inspiring countless other writers and artists, *Frankenstein* has fascinated for centuries, even inspiring the monster movies of the 1930s and 1940s. It is gay filmmaker James Whale's cinematic 1931 adaptation that gifted the monster his iconic bolt through the neck, and the movie is now read, in part, as Whale's frustration with anti-gay sentiment in 1930s America. LGBTQ+ academics are particularly enthralled by the monster, noting that he is ostracized for his inherent difference, transgressive body, sensitivity and power. To some, he is the ultimate queer villain, without the speedy gay walking pace and love of iced coffee. Seeing the monster as Frankenqueer throws a new light on the fascination between Victor Frankenstein and the creature, his brutish, 8-foot man-hunk. Might Shelley have guessed that her novel would ultimately be read as a queer text, or would she have been as surprised as Victor Frankenstein at his creation's other life?

In the early 19th century, upholding conservatism meant maintaining a balance between what was right, prim and proper and our monstrous, sloppy, inner selves. Politicians and lawmakers were in the beginnings of a gay panic, and writers and artists were at great pains to explore this fascinating tangle of sexless morality and the overwhelming urge to kick off your corset and let it all hang out. Some authors turned to classical queer villains like Dionysus, Pan and the maenads, letting their ancient hedonism serve as a warning to all those who might let their sexuality peek out. But, with *Frankenstein*, Shelley made the inner self real; all that monstrous lustiness, animalism and simmering queerness was suddenly within arm's reach – an early version of 'the calls are coming from inside the house'.

'When you're gay and grow up feeling like a hideous misfit, fully conscious that some believe your desires to be wicked and want to kill you for them, identifying with the Monster is hardly a stretch,' writes Charlie Fox in *T: The New York Times Style Magazine* (2017) in his piece examining *Frankenstein*'s forever-appeal to LGBTQ+ creatives. 'There's something about this story of unhallowed arts that makes it darkly resonant for queer artists beyond any other group,' he claims, pointing out that Victor Frankenstein's narration 'mimic[s] the rabid noise of a trans/homophobic chorus.'

From fears surrounding AI, the marvel of surgical transformation and the monster being birthed by a man, Shelley's novel is full of prescient ideas. But perhaps there is a kinder way to greet this LGBTQ+ villain: he is simply the product of what happens when society shuns difference. What might happen if our true, inner creatures were set free? Would we welcome them with open arms or chase them away with pitchforks? For now, let's accept this thoroughly queer monster. Frankenstein's monster? Steel your stitches, buff up your bolts and come through.

LUCIFER

The bewitchingly handsome devil himself

To St Paul's Cathedral in Liège, Belgium, and the year 1843, an auspicious time and place for Lucifer to finally reveal himself to be – quite literally – a sublime and extremely sexy devil. That year saw the installation of a series of gorgeous marble statues, each one celebrating a different saint, with the final piece depicting the *L'ange du mal*, the Angel of Evil. The artist who created them, commissioned six years previously, was sculptor Joseph Geefs, one of six gifted art-celeb brothers. After studying in Antwerp and Paris, Geefs was hot property: he was the Royal Sculptor of Belgium, winner of the Prix de Rome in 1836, and seemed to be the perfect, pious man to create the cathedral's most sacred pieces from his Brussels atelier. The statues were finally installed to much fanfare in 1843 but there was a problem. The Angel of Evil piece, a depiction of Lucifer himself, truly horrified cathedral leaders. Not because it was too monstrous, scaly or goat-headed, but because Geefs's evil angel – a semi-nude, muscle-bound, handsome human with wings, sitting coquettishly on a rock – looked, well, too god-damned desirable. (It turns out that Joseph had a penchant for mythological subjects, often with an erotic theme.)

Lucifer is Christianity's ultimate bad guy, synonymous with Satan and, to many, just another version of the devil himself (Lucifer is thought to be Satan's original, pre-fame name). To the Ancient Romans he was known as the Light-Bringer or Morning Star; in the Bible he is the simple serpent in the book of Genesis, and in the book of Isaiah he is the once-heavenly angel who falls from grace, careening through the sky and cast down to Earth. In Dante's *Inferno* (1314), he is less pretty and has morphed into a three-faced demon with bat wings under each chin, and in the film adaptation of Ira Levin's *Rosemary's Baby* (1968), he is the reptilian, yellow-eyed, clawed monster who chooses innocent Rosemary – whether she likes it or not – to be the mother of his earthly son. Wherever there is temptation, or at the very least, a sulphuric smell, there is Lucifer.

What was Joseph Geefs thinking in making this monster look so delicious? The local press reported that the statue was too sublime, distracting 'pretty penitent girls' – and boys, no doubt. Which brings us to the inherent queerness of this ancient evil being. According to fundamentalist religious types, the

Prince of Shadows is also, almost by default, the Patron Saint of Gays. With queerness forever at odds with faith, and countless memoirs and movies that unpick the all-too-common experience of LGBTQ+ people growing up in religious families and communities feeling unseen and unwanted, casting the devil as a queer temptation is a no-brainer. Gay Black hip-hop artist Lil Nas X knows this only too well. In the 2021 video for his unofficial coming out single, 'Montero (Call Me by Your Name)' he verily broke the internet with a fantastical, biblical-inspired fantasy that sees Lil Nas seduced by a snake, then executed before he slides down a stripper pole to Hell to seduce the devil himself. It caused such a stir, he claimed that the Black Entertainment Television Awards asked his team to 'confirm he wasn't a satanist or devil-worshipper' before booking him to perform the song on stage. He responded by finishing his electrifying live set with an on-stage man-on-man kiss.

Back in Liège, Bishop Van Bommel ordered the removal of Joseph's titillating sculpture and the commission passed to his brother, Guillaume Geefs. His own version, *Le génie du mal*, aka the Genius of Evil, was installed in 1848. But there was another problem: Guillaume's statue was just as fascinatingly beautiful as his brother's, if not more so. His Lucifer had the same perfectly ripped torso, but now his legs were slightly parted and one toned arm reached behind his head, his hand tousling his

own lustrous hair. Tricep flexed, Lucifer exposes his armpit, in what – in contemporary times – reads as the ultimate gay male selfie pose. And his bat-like wings? Updated with veins, giving a swollen, engorged feel to the piece. What devilry was this?

Joseph's original *L'ange du mal* was passed on after William II's death and in 2009 reached the Royal Museum of Fine Arts in Belgium. But Guillaume's version, the Lucifer of Liège, remains seductively at the pulpit at St Paul's Cathedral. He holds a crown and a broken sceptre, symbolizing his fall from grace; at his feet is an apple, bitten; chains bind him (giving the piece its uneasy BDSM feel); and, if you look closely, you can see a tiny set of horns peeping out from his thick, manly hair. This queer devil is, quite literally, horny.

LESTAT

Anne Rice's bisexual vampire rock star with one thing on his mind

There are many dark iterations of iconic vampire text *Interview with the Vampire*, but the master-tape version, Anne Rice's 1976 debut novel, has centuries-old Louis de Pointe du Lac – the titular vampire – narrate his incredible life to a writer in modern-day San Francisco. His tale of bawdy 1790s colonial New Orleans, where he is a white plantation owner, his voyage to the old world of Europe, his almost-daughter, Claudia, and the endless murders by fang, fire and sunlight all pale against Louis's memories of ponytailed nightmare Lestat de Lioncourt, aka the Brat Prince. The scene-stealing uber-vamp is Louis's maker, mentor and chaotic top, but he's jealous, petulant, impatient and dangerous, a truly amoral villain – and all the more fascinating for it.

For those who discovered Rice's *Vampire Chronicles* in the 1990s, it was Tom Cruise who set the tone for Lestat in Neil

Jordan's imperfect but lush 1994 film adaptation. Rice was nervous about the casting and couldn't imagine the *Risky Business* star being able to undertake the role, but Cruise gives his all to the eternal, befrilled party boy: it's a legendary performance with full jumping-up-and-down-on-Oprah's-couch energy. The on-screen love affair between Cruise's Lestat and Brad Pitt's Louis (all heavenly tousled hair and melancholy) makes *Interview* one of the gayest straight movies ever made: the queer subtext is as subtle as a stake through the heart. But it was decades later, in 2022, that the *Vampire Chronicles* Immortal Universe crawled out of its heteronormative coffin and got to work making good on all those half-whispered bisexual promises.

Need to see vampires having the gayest vampire sex imaginable? Almost 30 years after Neil Jordan's movie, AMC's 2022 series adaptation gets the pulse racing. This time, it's Australian actor Sam Reid in the Lestat role with British actor Jacob Anderson as Louis, a well-off, handsome but closeted Black man in 1910s New Orleans. Reid's Lestat is a delightfully WASPish and ethereally beautiful French brothel-owner, and the premier episode swings very, very gay. Their mutual attraction – instantaneous, electric – precedes a bare-butt-naked make-out session. The scene is passionate, incredibly queer and candlelit romantic; as Lestat bites Louis's neck, their sweaty, entwined bodies levitate. Eventually he turns Louis into a vampire, 'in a swoon of infatuation and white saviorism,' writes TV critic Inkoo Kang in *The New Yorker* (2022). The steamy AMC version also brings in the previously unexplored dimension of race, deliciously complicating the power dynamics with its realistic (and horrifying) version of old New Orleans at the height of Jim Crow. Lestat truly believes he is bestowing on Louis an ancient gift that will allow him to transcend everything, even bigotry. 'But it takes the Frenchman a long while to realize what his lover understands intuitively,' Kang writes. '[That] not even immortality supersedes race.' This is so often the case with poor Lestat; he is age-old yet has so much to learn.

With Louis's dissatisfaction and annoying moralism underpinned by religion (at one point he seeks forgiveness in church for his gay desire), things soon sour between the pair. But their toxic relationship remains passionate, with years-long monumental fallings-out repaired by Lestat's flirty provocations and moments of feverish chandelier-swinging. Lestat also deals with Louis's dull religious fixation in a very Lestat way – by viciously murdering two preachers, one of them via a gory superhero skull-punch.

Although Rice set up Lestat as the sexy antagonist in *Interview*, she clearly loved the character; and he became the throughline of the nine-book *Chronicles* and three crossover titles from her *Mayfair Witches* series, too. Rice sees him through numerous incarnations, from sensitive carer for his ailing father to embarrassing rock star to world-saver, making him far more morally complicated than the debut novel suggests. But it is still Lestat as the original, queer-edged Brat Prince who delights the most. He takes any opportunity for transgression, large or small. Reid's AMC version has supernatural super-speed – portrayed on screen as if time has slowed down – allowing Lestat to cheat at poker games. And in another scene, Lestat's love of music and theatre is overshadowed by his displeasure at a disappointing performance and he murders an opera singer for having limited range. This is the true gift of Lestat: with his perfectly toned vampire thighs, he straddles the uneasy space between playfulness and passion, respect for life and the thrill of the kill, the freedom of queer love and the instinct to destroy everyone he cares for. 'Evil is always possible,' writes Rice in *Interview*. 'And goodness is eternally difficult.'

MRS DANVERS
The OG queer housekeeper of Daphne du Maurier

For ultimate queer villainy of the dark and brooding kind, all roads lead to Manderley. The sprawling country-house estate is the perfect place for a young, naive newlywed and her wealthy older husband, Maxim de Winter, to continue their sun- and fun-filled love affair. But soon after the unnamed narrator arrives, full of hope and romantic ideals, she discovers that her new home is a living mausoleum to Maxim's just-dead wife, Rebecca. And there is another who haunts Manderley: solemn housekeeper Mrs Danvers, torn apart by loss, unable to articulate her pain and fizzing with repressed sexuality. The narrator hopes to find solace within the de Winter estate, but to Danvers, this gold-digging strumpet is practically dancing on the dead woman's grave.

This is the setup for Daphne du Maurier's 1938 Gothic novel *Rebecca*, the writer's most popular title – although one she blithely dismissed as 'just a phase' in a TV interview in 1971. Literary phase or not, it is a masterclass in dark obfuscation, plot twists and Gothic thrills. And like all the best, most audacious fictional narratives, much of it was drawn from real life. Like her heroine, Daphne du Maurier also married young, after a whirlwind three-month-long romance, and her husband, Frederick Browning, wasn't quite the man he purported to be. At the time of the novel's publication, the fight for women's rights in the UK, particularly around marriage, were at fever pitch, with women having only won the right to divorce in 1937, and romance novels were booming: *Rebecca* was an instant hit. But right away, readers wondered about a certain queerness in the text. Just what exactly was the relationship between Danvers – who the narrator masculinizes with the nickname Danny – and the first Mrs de Winter? And what might explain the housekeeper's obsessive preservation of her late mistress's reputation, gorgeous furs and used undies?

Many critics have long been reluctant to accept that du Maurier wrote Danvers and Rebecca with a lesbian subtext, and it is true that overt explorations of queer sexuality were pretty much absent from bestselling books of the time. But, if du Maurier's *Rebecca* begins to tentatively question what society deems acceptable in terms of female sexuality, then Alfred Hitchcock answers. Just two years after the book's publication, the director released his iconic movie version and 'Danny' Danvers became *Rebecca*'s villain on the big screen in a barnstorming and Academy Award-nominated performance by Judith Anderson. On screen, her Danvers is both painfully restrained and hilariously camp and creepy; and in her scenes with our heroine (Joan Fontaine), her looming physicality suggests sadistic qualities: she just loves to watch the second Mrs de Winter sob. Running Manderley and its staff with utter precision, Danvers is the eternal headmistress, and there is a through-line from Hitchcock's Danvers to similar queer-edged characters. Both the iconic Mrs Appleyard in *Picnic at Hanging Rock* (1975) and even Miss Trunchbull in *Matilda* (1996, 2022) have Danvers's lesbian energy.

Just like in the novel, Anderson's housekeeper slowly tortures the narrator, manipulating and gaslighting her into embarrassments and upsets. Finally, Danvers near-murders her by encouraging the second Mrs De Winter to take her own life. As the mystery is unpicked, Rebecca is revealed to have been somewhat of a monster herself, cruel and manipulative and possibly psychopathic. But more contemporary readings suggest that perhaps that's what being trapped in a marriage to the ultimately nasty Maxim de Winter does to a woman.

Du Maurier took part in a BBC radio interview in 1977 with a fellow author who, at the time, was poised to write an unsolicited prequel to *Rebecca*. Du Maurier seemed to politely warn them off using the following example: she herself had discovered evidence of an affair between King Charles I and Oliver Cromwell but had decided not to publish it. Was du Maurier issuing a warning not to portray Danvers as a lesbian? Or was she confirming that Danny was something of a Gentleman Jack?

But then, a queer plot twist. 'After du Maurier died in 1989,' reports the Lavender Menace blog (2020), 'her biographers were able to be truthful about her life. It emerged that she was bisexual and had fallen in love with her publisher's elegant wife, Ellen Doubleday. She had also had an affair with the actress Gertrude Lawrence (though Lawrence's family deny the idea to this day).' What's more, the same blog reports that in letters, 'du Maurier compared Doubleday to Rebecca', and suggests that 'perhaps du Maurier herself, through her passion for Doubleday, had come to see Rebecca differently.'

The Danvers of du Maurier's novel and the Danvers of Hitchcock's movie have melded together in the LGBTQ+ consciousness, creating a single fascinating character with a complex sexuality. The idea that du Maurier herself was bisexual truly throws a queer light on *Rebecca* and the villainous character who, after years of buttoned-up repression, ultimately burns Manderley to the ground.

IRENA DUBROVNA

The tragic feline femme fatale of the Cat People

Meet Irena Dubrovna (Simone Simon), a beautiful fashion illustrator from Serbia and glamorous newcomer to 1940s New York City society, living and loving under the shadow of unspeakable paranoia. She is unable to have sex with her handsome new husband, Oliver, her psychiatrist thinks she is recovering from childhood trauma, and there's another problem: Oliver seems to have taken a shine to his pretty, uncomplicated assistant, Alice. It's a catastrophe.

Everything about Irena is subtly threatening. She's the anti-all-American girl: brunette when she should be blonde, bourgeois when she should be provincial, an immigrant with an accent when she should be American, born-and-bred. Even Irena's job as a fashion illustrator underlines her otherness; it's elite and mystic to everyday audiences. Oh, and – spoiler alert – she could be a part-time black panther. Convinced she is a descendent of an ancient race of cat people, she believes that a moment of true passion will turn her into a predator, who will then maul the object of her desire. And if that wasn't enough to scare the audience, Irena is also queer coded.

Cat People is the 1942 supernatural horror starring Simone Simon, Kent Smith and Jane Rudolph and has forever been catnip to queer film historians. Visually, *Cat People* set the template for spooky lighting effects and shadow play, and although it was released in the midst of cinema's monster phase, the movie borrowed the nihilistic worldview, femme fatale and murderous goings-on of classic noir cinema. Like many movies of the period, *Cat People* was made under the Hays Code, conservative guidelines enforced by the major studios that forbade overt sexual content on screen and presented a challenge for film studios, who were known to hide anything truly tasty in the subtext instead. It's here that *Cat People*'s queerness lives: underneath the monster madness there is a tragic tale of otherness.

As things worsen for Irena, strange things start to happen. At her wedding celebration a feline-like Serbian woman, captivated by her, calls her 'my sister' and a mysterious animal stalks Alice. The film seems to ask: is Irena a victim of her own paranoia and sexual dysfunction or is she secretly a panther? But the true horror of *Cat People* is Irena's implied queerness, itself a dimension of female sexuality. After all, what could be more frightening than a woman who desperately avoids heterosexual sex and, in fact, might prefer – whisper it – lesbian love? A woman who does not need a man? In the world of *Cat People*, this is a truly monstrous idea.

Like so many queer people, Irena knows that her inner identity might render her an outcast and so she keeps her true self hidden. But there are signs: the feline woman who approaches her at the restaurant seems to out Irena, leaving her terrified and embarrassed; she's described as 'odd' by other diners and goes home and scrubs herself. 'This fear of association and discovery would certainly resonate with a gay and lesbian audience in this time period,' points out pop-culture writer Elizabeth Erwin on the website *Horror Homeroom* (2015). 'On the surface,' she continues, 'these exchanges appear innocuous but to a queer audience in the 1940s, a female being labeled "odd" would function in much the same way as a gay man being called a "sissy." ' Erwin points out that Irena's tragic bathtub scene is her attempt to 'scrub herself clean of the label and is a clear indicator that Irena recognizes (and loathes) the otherness she sees in herself.' And in an earlier scene, Irena describes the original cat people, the ancient community from which she descends, as having done 'dreadful things', making them seem sexually perverse – *just like her*.

Things cannot stay as they are. Oliver wants Irena to truly embody her role as his presumably straight wife and she agrees to visit psychiatrist Dr Judd, but her mysterious disappearances are increasing and a mystery cat is on the prowl. When Oliver announces that he is in love with all-American Alice and wants a divorce, it pushes Irena over the edge. She finally accepts a kiss from Dr Judd (his attempts to 'cure' his patient might just mark him out as the real monster of this story). She knows it will be the end of her – and him. Her worst fear is realized: she magically shapeshifts into a black panther, mauls creepy Judd to death and – in cat form – is soon killed herself. Irena choses death rather than a lonely life as her true self, and the men in her life have truly failed in their attempts to tame her. Irena's lifeless human body is found where a panther was thought to have been killed and, the villain vanquished, Oliver comforts Alice: heteronormality is restored. This queer monster is defeated not with a roar, but a miaow.

THE MASTER
(AND THE MISTRESS)

The dual-gender Time Lord
villain of *Doctor Who*

'Would it help you focus if I extracted some of your vital organs and made a lovely soup?' asks Missy, imploring her grandstanding foe, Razor, to hurry up already. The endlessly patient, jauntily dressed, intergalactic big bad of *Doctor Who* is in a bind. It's the climax of episode 275, 'World Enough and Time' (2017), and she's on a spaceship about to win dominion over the Earth – only her captor has a weapon pointed right at her. Just then, Razor rips off his disguise and, somehow, he is Missy's male self, beamed in from an earlier timeline. It's an astonishing twist. He is – they are – both the Master and the Mistress, the deadliest villain the universe has ever seen. Missy is in shock. 'Give us a kiss,' he says. It is very weird, very *Doctor Who*, and very queer indeed.

Doctor Who is the galaxy's longest-running sci-fi TV show, remaining one of the most successful and one of the queerest. It premiered in 1963 and, even with its sad off-air period from 1989 to 2005, it still beats *Star Trek* by a year. LGBTQ+ creatives have been involved in *Doctor Who* from the very beginning (the director of the first-ever episode, Waris Hussein, is gay); and for a show that was once criticized for upholding a conservative point of view, it became a masterclass in representation. *Queer as Folk* creator Russell T Davies is showrunner; Ncuti Gatwa, the Rwandan-Scottish queer actor from *Sex Education*, is the Fifteenth Doctor; and *Heartstopper*'s Yasmin Finney plays a trans character. And in the wider Whoniverse there's all manner of queerness: brash bisexual Captain Jack Harkness, lesbian companion Bill Potts, Madame Vastra and Jenny Flint (a lesbian Sherlock and Watson whose passionate queer kiss was cut from an episode for Singaporean audiences), and a pansexual Fourteenth Doctor played by Jodie Whittaker.

As Moriarty to his Holmes, the Master is, officially, the Doctor's ultimate enemy. He first appeared in 1971 and over the years has been played by more than 12 actors, including John Simm and, in 'World Enough and Time', Michelle Gomez as Missy. But their aeons-long frisson is complicated. If the Doctor is the chaotic, occasionally gender-changing, English-accented social-justice warrior who zigzags through time and space, it's the Master who keeps him in check, makes him laugh and tries to lure him over to the dark side.

Like any nemesis and their obsession, there is an undeniable connection between the two. Both are Time Lords a million light years from home; and when they are not trying to kill each other, they are trying to save each other. It's 'a friendship older than your civilization. And infinitely more complex,' explains Missy to the Doctor's then companion, Clara (who, at one point, kissed Jane Austen). It's like Missy thinks the Doctor belongs to her.

Over the last decade, the gender of both the Doctor and the Master has tended to flip-flop, creating new versions of the same relationship. When Missy appeared as the first female version of the Master, it seemed to throw new light on the Doctor and the Master's past encounters. In 'The Sound of Drums' (2007), the Master says to the Doctor: 'Are you asking me out on a date?' At the time it sounded sarcastic, but was it really? And when the Doctor and Missy passionately kiss in 'Dark Water' (2014), she lunges at him, pressing him against the wall, his hand flailing while Clara looks away, embarrassed. It appears the pair are finally acting on a lifelong desire. But with so many encounters over the years, and so much queer opportunity, why couldn't they have kissed when they were both male? The moment is confusing and comic; and, while the scene is ostensibly a man and a woman messily making out, it sent shockwaves through the fanbase: this was a queer kiss if ever there was one.

SKELETOR

The cackling cartoon villain of the queerest animated show ever made

In the darkest recesses of the internet there exists a four-minute fan video of He-Man alter ego Prince Adam, redubbed and performing an emotional Euro-club remix of 1990s mega-hit 'What's Up?' by 4 Non Blondes. In 'Fabulous Secret Powers', Adam's choppy blond bob, just like gay icon Peter Berlin's, sways as he sings mournfully; his outfit – lavender leggings, furry purple boots and a clingy, rose-pink blouse – fits his body like a glove. Viewed more than 150 million times, it is just as it sounds: the gayest thing ever.

The creators Jay Allen and Ryan Haines, aka Slackcircus, first dropped their affectionate homage to legendary 1980s cartoon series *He-Man and the Masters of the Universe* in 2005 and, in doing so, revealed something we had known all along. The iconic rainbow-hued cartoon and muscle-bound Mattel action-figure line was overtly queer coded, and He-Man and his archnemesis Skeletor were less fighters than star-crossed lovers.

In the original animated show spanning 130 episodes from 1983 to 1985, the action takes place on faraway planet Eternia, where He-Man, the secret identity of Prince Adam, and his barely dressed friends defend the sacred Castle Grayskull from evil Skeletor and his cronies. In each episode, Prince Adam's transformation scene seems to reaffirm the show's queerness. As Sam Anderson writes breathlessly at online magazine *Slate* (11 May 2006), '[He-Man's] clothes fall off, his voice drops a full octave, his skin turns from vanilla to nut brown, his giant sword starts gushing energy [. . .] next, he typically runs around seizing space-wands with glowing knobs and fabulously straddling giant rockets. [And] he hangs out with people called Fisto and Ram Man.'

With his impossibly muscly and lithe physique, Skeletor is He-Man's apparent foe, known for his catty put-downs and trademark cackle. He's the Halloween version of the He-Man's Castro Clone, the gay male subculture prevalent in the 1980s, and is by far the show's most fascinating and fun character. But what Anderson calls *He-Man*'s 'hilarious accidental homo-eroticism' might not have been quite so accidental after all. Erika Scheimer was vocal director of He-Man spin-off *She-Ra* at Filmation Studios, run by her father, Lou Scheimer. She remembers having to assert herself to cast the voice actor she wanted for She-Ra. 'I was a strong female voice myself,' she told Prism Comics in 2014, 'and – guess what? – I happened to be gay. Does that make any difference about anything? I'll tell you one thing, it didn't matter, because Filmation was one of the gayest places in town.'

If the animated series is queer coded, then the messy, 1987 live-action movie – starring Swedish sexpot Dolph Lundgren as He-Man and Frank Langella as a languorous, unhinged Skeletor – is an ersatz S&M love story between its protagonist and antagonist. 'Watching *Masters of the Universe* with adult eyes revealed the film to be a tragic unrequited romance between He-Man and Skeletor,' claimed Adam B Vary in a BuzzFeed article (22 October 2013). At one point, Skeletor is about to win dominance over planet Earth but all he cares about is He-Man, Vary points out. He wants to see him 'kneeling at his feet'; and, when the object of his desire is finally captured, stripped to a pair of leather briefs and whipped, Skeletor can barely contain himself, gripping his staff and wriggling with pleasure on his throne.

Slackcircus's 'Secret Fabulous Powers' meme, a new Masters of the Universe collectors' toy range and a generation of gay Comic Con fanboys all helped keep the brand alive, and in 2021, He-Man returned in *Masters of the Universe: Revelation*. The

Netflix animated series stars Mark Hamil as Skeletor, Chris Wood as He-Man and Sarah Michelle Gellar as He-Man's friend Teela, and was created by He-Man mega-fans Rob David and Tim Sheridan, who are happily aware of the brand's queer power. But, in their version, the underlying tension that was such a transgressive element of the show in 1980s conservative Reagan-era America has evolved. Instead, the show seems to be about hidden identities and the more general pain and pleasure of being your true self. As Sheridan explained to online magazine *Queerty* in 2021, the show sets out to explore certain questions: 'What is it about those secrets that we keep – our "fabulous secret powers" – what happens if we keep those secrets too long? How can they fester? What effect do they have?'

And yet, the specifically queer power of Grayskull lingers on in its LGBTQ+ fanbase, the endless gay Skeletor memes and in Etsy merch (the Skeletor-themed 'Lurk, Laugh, Loathe' sew-on patch for the win). The characters will always have a touch of queerness, just as He-Man tells us in the original 1980s series, 'I feel the bony finger of Skeletor!'

FREDDY KRUEGER

The blade-clawed supernatural slasher with chaotic top energy

'He's inside me,' pleads Jesse, the hormonal teen haunted by the villain with the bladed glove, 'and he wants to take me again!' The desperate character – high-school handsome, blond, undeniable twink energy – is possessed by Freddy Krueger (Robert Englund), the iconic antagonist of *A Nightmare on Elm Street*, the supernatural-slasher franchise that splattered its way through nine movies in the 1980s, 1990s and beyond. *Freddy's Revenge* (1985) is the sequel to the wildly successful original movie and, although created for a mainstream audience, has earned a reputation for being one of the queerest horror movies ever made.

Following on from the original movie, Jesse Walsh (Mark Patton) and his family move into a house on Elm Street, the site of Freddy's demise five years earlier. But it seems the monster wasn't truly slayed; and Jesse is soon possessed by Krueger, who infects the dreams of his victims and, in the high-school teen's case, uses him to kill others. From the beginning, *Freddy's Revenge* is a queer one. Jesse is too shy to flirt with girls, enjoys a little rough and tumble with new friend Grady, and – in a bid to stay awake and immune from Freddy's powers – walks the streets at night and wanders into a gay leather bar. Krueger isn't afraid to flirt: he looms large, toying with Jesse, conjuring sexual tension with his male prey, tenderly tousling his hair; he's sassy and camp and endlessly creepy. In this way, *Freddy's Revenge* swaps the Final Girl (the horror trope in which a female character always survives, at least until the finale) for a Final Boy, subverting the tits 'n' ass overt sexualization of horror's nubile scream queens. Audiences well-versed in the eroticism of the genre still had their expectations met, but in a truly unexpected way: here was male nudity, bare-bum-cheeked male-on-male horseplay, a high-school gym coach in a leather bar, Jesse in his tighty whities, and haunted towel flicks in a steamy locker room.

Patton has a complicated relationship with the movie. Its gay themes were developed on set via production rewrites, leaving Patton – who is gay, but was not out at the time – increasingly uncomfortable. A scripted scene in which Jesse is invited to fellate Freddy's bladed glove was thrown out on Patton's request, but the film still screams out its queerness (and Freddy still gets to caress Jesse's lips with his appendage). In one scene, Jesse is surrounded by phallic candles, his naked torso splashed with white wax, and an awkward make-out scene between Jesse and his friend Lisa ends with Jesse running to handsome Grady's bedroom. Jesse climbs on top of him, desperate to tell him about Freddy's hold over him. 'He's inside me,' moans Jesse, to which Grady replies, 'And you want to sleep with me?'

Although he had already played a gay character on stage, Patton was at the beginning of his career and had been pressured to keep his own sexuality a secret. He'd been told to take a female companion to his Broadway show's opening night and to dress, well, straight. In the mid-1980s, the stakes were incredibly high: 'By that point, AIDS was all around me,' Patton said in an interview with *HIV Plus* magazine in 2013. 'Everyone I knew was getting sick.' Increasingly, critics and audiences were aware of the *Freddy's Revenge*'s queerness, but its makers were holding fast: this was absolutely not a gay movie. It didn't help that, for decades, writer David Chaskin denied that *Freddy's Revenge* had any purposefully queer leanings, while others claimed that it was Patton's performance that gave the film its gay edge. But eventually Chaskin seemed to soften: 'I feigned ignorance,' he finally told *BuzzFeed News* in 2016. 'My movie was being outed and I didn't know how I felt about that.'

Nightmare 2 was queer all along. Patton was vindicated, and among Chaskin's inspirations were homophobia, the AIDS epidemic and the gross-out fear of queerness prevalent in *Nightmare*'s core audience: teenage boys.

If Patton has a complicated relationship with *Freddy's Revenge*, the movie itself has its own demons. Recreating Freddy as a queer villain relies on tired, stereotypical tropes: the older gay man seducing the innocent teen, the endless innuendo . . . Doesn't this maintain homophobia rather than dismantle it? But time has been kind to *A Nightmare on Elm Street 2: Freddy's Revenge*. With its queerness hidden in plain sight for so many years, it has been reclaimed by a slew of LGBTQ+ horror fans who now delight at the movie's heavy-handed approach to sexuality. What in 1985 might have seemed a subtle, blink-and-you'll-miss-it gay subtext, is now seen for what it truly is: queer magic slashing and splattering across the screen.

FRANK-N-FURTER

The world's most evil *Cabaret*-style alien bisexual scientist

Somewhere, at this very moment, *The Rocky Horror Picture Show* is glittering on screen. Patricia Quinn's mouth – blood-red, disembodied – is lip-synching to the opening number, 'Science-Fiction/Double Feature', each word pure cinematic history. The camp classic musical has been in queer rotation since its release in 1975; and singing along, dressing as its characters, getting Little Nell tattoos and perfecting the dramatic pause in the line 'I see you shiver with antici . . . pation' is a rite of passage for countless LGBTQ+ young people. They find kinship in *Rocky Horror*'s cast of oddballs, misfits and kinksters and in its transgressive drag sensibility. But the movie belongs to its fishnet-and-basque-wearing bisexual male lead, Frank-N-Furter, one of the queerest villains of them all.

The joyful 1970s stage show and its cinematic adaptation are loosely based on Mary Shelley's *Frankenstein* and are a love letter to B-movies, horror, science fiction and kink. The story follows all-American couple Brad and Janet (Barry Bostwick and Susan Sarandon) as they seek help in Castle Transylvania late one night. Their host, scientist Frank-N-Furter (Tim Curry, otherworldly charming), is poised to reveal his latest Franken-project – only his version of the monster is a blond, muscle-bound hunk in tiny gold hotpants. But Furter also has designs on the recently engaged couple, leaving them thoroughly and breathlessly queered.

Like *All About Eve* (1950), *Cabaret* (1972) and *Burlesque* (2010), *Rocky Horror* is still considered required viewing for all newcomers to the LGBTQ+ fam, but culture has shifted since 1975. The movie has its own complex lore and enduring fandom, and different decades have found Frank-N-Furter more transgressive than others. The movie was entered into the Library of Congress in 2005; and its most recent big-budget reboot was commissioned by the conservative, right-wing television network Fox. The 2016 adaptation had Nickelodeon and Disney stars playing Brad and Janet, trans actor Laverne Cox playing Frank-N-Furter (a character she has loved since her own college days) and *Hocus Pocus* director Kenny Ortega at the helm. At the time, some of Fox's audience bristled at the idea and it certainly had culture writer Alexa Moutevelis biting her bottom lip: 'What was Fox thinking when it aired *The Rocky*

Horror Picture Show?' she scolded via right-wing media watchdog site NewsBusters. 'This is wildly inappropriate material for minors – and most people, really – to begin with, so I don't know how this remake got off the drawing board at Fox.' It takes some chops being on the political right of Fox, but the network soon caught up: at the time of writing, Moutevelis is now an editor at Fox News Digital. Indeed, it's hard to think of any right-wing platform commissioning the show today; the 'Sweet Transvestite' is transgressive again.

'I know of a lot of people whose lives were saved by this movie,' says Larry Viezel, president of *The Rocky Horror Picture Show* Official Fan Club, in an interview with the BBC's Larushka Ivan-Zadeh in 2020. 'Especially for those in the LGBT community, it's a place where they could be themselves.' Describing the communal nature of *Rocky Horror* screenings, full of audience call-backs and props thrown at the screen, Viezel says, 'For a lot of people, *Rocky Horror* is like their home, it's their connection to everybody – all their friends.' But, back to the real villain of the piece, Frank-N-Furter, and his everlasting queer magic. In turn, Brad and Janet fall under his spell, and both are seemingly deflowered by the alien being (spoiler alert: Furter turns out to be from another planet). This appears to be Frank-N-Furter's real power: he may be unsuccessful in his Frankenstein experiments, but he is the great liberator, pushing others' boundaries, revealing pleasure and flinging open their closet doors whether they want to come out or not. Perhaps it is this sentiment that has made the movie and stage show so timeless. Furter's enduring line, sung over and over in the movie's finale, is a resonant one for queer people: 'Don't dream it, be it.'

BEETLEJUICE
Tim Burton's bi-furious bio-exterminator

Tim Burton has a thing for outsiders. The delightful characters who front his movies are almost always pushed to the edge of mainstream society and threatened for their difference, yet they are ultimately admired for their kookiness, too. Some, like Edward Scissorhands, are merely misunderstood, tragic victims of the crushing expectations of social conformity. Others are just total asshats: meet Beetlejuice, the villainous bisexual, pansexual, everything-sexual ghost, bio-exterminator and all-round gross-out artist.

Beetlejuice (1988) was Burton's second movie, a surreal comic horror known for its sharp performances and social satire where the oddballs win out and the yuppies get their comeuppance. The movie's spooktacular villain is played with foul-mouthed, lounge-lizard energy by a deranged Michael Keaton – all black-and-white-striped suit, green hair and conman spiel – who gets a total of 20 minutes on-screen time but still steals the show. The set-up has Burton's adorable but painfully vanilla newlyweds, Barbara and Adam Maitland (Geena Davis and Alec Baldwin), die in the middle of renovating their breathtakingly twee country home in Connecticut. As novice ghosts, they are unable to scare off an obnoxious new family from their home and so, against advice from an afterlife desk clerk, they employ Beetlejuice's bio-extermination services to 'exorcise the living'. But his unorthodox way of working means that the plan to evict the Deetzes – Charles, Delia and Charles's cute but morbid daughter Lydia – create deathly problems for them all.

At the time, Beetlejuice himself didn't scream 'queer' – in fact, with all his leching, he had more in common with the contemporary villains of 'me too' than with queer-coded demons – but the slowly evolving Beetleverse had other ideas. A *Beetlejuice* cartoon ran from 1989 to 1991 and focused on the uneasy friendship between Lydia and 'Juice and that, in turn, informed a reboot in 2019 when *Beetlejuice* was resurrected again. Standby for the razzamatazz of *Beetlejuice* on Broadway, a stage musical that won itself a slew of award nominations and a book, written by Scott Brown and Anthony King, pushing 'Juice a little further along the Kinsey scale. The Beetlejuice played by Alex Brightman is bisexual or pansexual, 'kisses Barbara, he kisses Adam. In the movie, he's portrayed a little more predatorial. In this [adaptation], he's just enamoured with people,' the actor said to *Variety* (2019) after the show's opening, 'I'm loving it.'

Whether its eponymous antihero is bisexual or not, *Beetlejuice* has a rather queer history. The original narrative might just draw on Oscar Wilde's 1887 short story 'The Canterville Ghost', about an American family who move into an English country house haunted by Sir Simon de Canterville, a character thought to be a substitute for Wilde. Theatrical and finicky, Canterville keeps to the shadows, wanders only at night and is persecuted for much of the story. 'The Canterville Ghost' also seems to have its own gay character: Washington, the eldest son, who 'was a rather good-looking young man' and 'well known as an excellent dancer', as Wilde wrote. 'Gardenias and the peerage were his only weaknesses', which is clearly a late 1800s literary version of 'Is he, you know?' Burton's Beetlejuice is a different creature to Wilde's Canterville from a century earlier, but both characters are true outsiders: who knows which ghostly goings-on inspired the screenwriters and Burton himself?

There are other *Beetlejuice* characters that don't quite fit in. Lydia is often thought of as a character with a queer edge: she's a Goth, is mourning the death of her mother, and in the musical tells us, 'I myself am strange and unusual.' Elsewhere, queer representation in *Beetlejuice* the movie is, well . . . It's complicated. Say hello to Otho, Delia's interior designer (to whom she is embarrassingly in thrall), friend and psychic advisor: snobbish, narcissistic and larger than life – and clearly coded as gay. If the Maitlands are somewhat stuck in time as the perfect apple-pie American couple, then Otho is a caricature of a waspish 1950s gay man: it's disappointing. And yet, he gives one of the movie's most memorable performances.

In Leah Schnelbach's 'An Ode to *Beetlejuice*'s Otho' (*Tor. com*, 1 August 2019), she sees the character as almost beyond sexuality: 'Otho is unmarried,' Schnelbach reminds us, and 'he might be queer? Actor Glenn Shadix was openly gay at a time when that was even less easy than it is now [. . .] We never know for sure *because it doesn't matter.*' Schnelbach points out that while the other adults are part of couples or 'heteronormative pairings [. . .] Otho is a free agent. A spirit of chaos.' It's true that Otho-lovers sense a little unfairness at play in *Beetlejuice*; the character is treated badly and ultimately humiliated by Beetlejuice, who defrocks him (turning his luxury designer outfit into a cheap leisure suit), following which Otho shrieks girlishly and runs away, seemingly unable to cope, and we never see him again. For Schnelbach this punchline rings hollow: Otho is punished but hasn't broken any rule; doesn't he deserve a happier ending? If Beetlejuice is our queer villain, then Otho, the 'spirit of chaos', might just be the movie's hero.

PENNYWISE

Stephen King's grotesque drain-dwelling clown villain

In 1986, legendary horror novelist Stephen King conjured a monster into being. After a long line of nightmarish antagonists, from a telekinetic prom queen to a Plymouth Fury with a taste for human flesh, King's Pennywise the dancing clown seemed an easy reach: everyone's scared of clowns, right? But the drain-dwelling character in King's novel, *It* – unhinged, grotesque and unbelievably camp – was a terrifying version of something safe and familiar, a freak from the fairground, and soon seeped into the American consciousness as one of the nation's all-time most frightening monsters.

Thanks to *It* and its various on-screen and off-screen adaptations, Pennywise pops up everywhere. He haunts Comic Cons, Gay Christmas (i.e., Halloween) parties and drag shows, and he's even been 'shipped' with unlikely queer meme star the Babadook (see page 193). JoJo Siwa danced in full Penny-drag on the 2021 season of *Dancing with the Stars*; and a recent scientific study, 'Fear of clowns: an investigation into the aetiology of coulrophobia' (*Frontiers of Psychology*, 2023) opens with a delicious Pennywise quote.

Set in the late 1950s in small-town Maine, King's novel sees a group of scrappy outsider kids known as the Losers Club terrorized by Pennywise. An alternating narrative set in the present day (then the mid-1980s) sees the Losers all grown up and about to face the same foe all over again. It is a shapeshifting creature that can transform into its victim's worst nightmare (which feels like a character from every queer house-share ever). Its guises include one character's murdered little brother, Georgie, and another's abusive husband, a werewolf, a mummy, the Creature from the Black Lagoon, a swarm of winged leeches and a giant, crawling, gooey eye, but It generally spends his downtime as Pennywise, the carnival clown.

Away from King's stomach-churning supernatural-horror scenes, *It* is a heart-wrenching read and an exploration of how childhood trauma and bullying reverberates into your adult years. The novel also draws from a horrific and violent anti-gay murder that rocked King's own Maine community in 1984.

Perhaps it was *It*'s first screen adaptation that marked Pennywise out as a little queer. In the cult two-part 1990 ABC miniseries *It* directed by horror-movie maestro Tommy Lee

Wallace, Pennywise was played by Tim Curry. Curry was a huge
Hollywood name, and *It* producers certainly had eyes for his
Frank-N-Furter (see page 141). His barnstorming performance
in *The Rocky Horror Picture Show* (1975), the queerest musical
science-fiction B-movie parody ever created, meant that he was
already known and loved by a generation of misfits and
midnight moviegoers. He brought a transgressive exuberance
to the role of Pennywise, adding a little Frank-N-Furter camp.

Hindi network Zee TV wrung 52 episodes out of King's
idea in 1998, and then, almost two decades later, came Andy
Muschietti's big-screen, big-budget 'duology', *It Chapter One*
(2017) and *It Chapter Two* (2019) with Bill Skarsgård in the
clown suit. Skarsgård's Pennywise is legendary, he's lithe,
sinuous and 'refreshingly weird', says Dani di Placido, in her
review of *Chapter One* (Forbes.com, 9 September 2017). 'He
doesn't appear remotely human,' she continues; 'he behaves
like an interdimensional creature, a demonic predator taking
the form of a clown.'

Chapter Two earned itself controversy. The extended
opening scene shows the torture and murder of a young gay
man, Adrian, at the hands of anti-gay thugs, and it is truly
horrific. At the time, Jeffrey Bloomer called it a 'gay-bashing
scene' exploiting a 'ghastly real-life killing for a cheap shock,
delivered without context or any clear thematic underpinning'

(online magazine *Slate*, 5 September 2019). Although the scene was dropped from the ABC Tim Curry adaptation, it might not have been a surprise for fans of the book; the same chapter opening plays out there. The 'real-life killing' Bloomer talks of is that of Charlie Howard, who was attacked and murdered in Bangor, Maine by three teenage boys in 1984 – in part, for wearing a flamboyant hat.

In both the book and *Chapter Two*, the scene is startling – like Charlie's own story, which, at the time, rocked Maine and clearly had a deep effect on King. But in both King's book and in Muschietti's movie, Adrian is a tragic hero, even if the story feels a little incongruous. This is all personal for Dr Charlie Allbright, author of *Stephen King's It: Culture and the Clown* (2019). On the night he signed a contract to write his Stephen King book, Allbright was 'assaulted and left for dead for wearing a flamboyant hat – a trilby with feathers in it,' he wrote in a piece defending the inclusion of the scene in *The Guardian* in 2019. 'The attackers asked me if I was queer.' Allbright points out that *It* star Jessica Chastain defended the scene: 'We can't pretend that [anti-gay violence] doesn't still exist,' she told *Variety*, and Allbright sees it as an integral element. 'By weaving the representation of an actual murder into his story,' he writes, 'King suggests *It*'s horror results from the license some think they have to perpetuate violence.'

PINHEAD

Horror supremo Clive Barker's queerest and creepiest creation

Since the early 1980s, the novels and short-story collections of British author, poet and artist Clive Barker have been the starting point for endless adaptations, from cult movies like *Candyman* (1992, 2021) to gory video games. His early writing kickstarted the splatterpunk horror movement with all its unexpected queer-edged eroticism, BDSM iconography and stomach-churning ultra-violence. Barker is known for his terrifying, visually unique hybrid monsters (think body modification, pierced nips, tight pleather onesies), but one creation has long haunted all his work. Meet Elliot Spencer, a soldier from WWI who happens upon a magical puzzle box. It transports him to a hellish dimension where he is a slave to the pain and pleasure of S&M, becomes the leader of the fetishy demonic Cenobites and ends up with a grid of pins stuck into his undead flesh. Spencer was officially known as the Hell

Priest, but Barker's fans had another name for their favourite queer villain: Pinhead.

By the mid-1980s, there were two movies based on Barker's work ('abominations', he called them in *The Guardian* in 2017) and he decided to direct one himself. He scraped together a relatively tiny budget and set to work making his own haunted-house movie based on his novella *The Hellbound Heart* (1986). The script (working title: *Sadomasochists from Beyond the Grave*) introduced the Cenobites, Barker's interdimensional ghouls that were beckoned by the solving of an enchanted puzzle box and had a penchant for torturing their prey. *A Nightmare on Elm Street* (1984) had been a game-changer for the horror genre and Barker's movie monsters needed an iconic look to better Freddy Krueger's bladed glove and striped sweater. Barker took inspiration from his own fascination with the burgeoning queer S&M scene. 'The look of the Cenobites, such as the pins in their leader's head, was inspired by S&M clubs,' said Barker in *The Guardian*. 'There was an underground club called Cellblock 28 in New York that had a very hard S&M night [. . .] It was the first time I ever saw people pierced for fun [. . .] The austere atmosphere definitely informed Pinhead.' Barker's *Hellraiser* was released in 1987 and Pinhead, played by Barker's old theatre friend Doug Bradley, became the movie's USP.

Even as far back as 1991, Ken Tucker had called Barker the 'grandaddy' of splatterpunk in *The New York Times*. 'Basically, splatterpunk bears the same relationship to horror fiction that punk rock did to rock-and-roll,' he writes. 'It is a radical gesture that shakes up the genre.' Pinhead certainly did just that, earning himself nine sequels and a full *Hellraiser* reboot in 2022. You can see Clive Barker's influence – and Pinhead's, too – everywhere, from Guillermo del Toro's *Pan's Labyrinth* (2006) to the cyberpunk *Matrix* universe created by filmmakers the Wachowskis (who, incidentally, wrote for Barker's Marvel Comics series *Razorline* back in the day). And yet Barker tried again and again to bump him off, finally managing it in his novel *The Scarlet Gospels* (2015), in which Pinhead, and all of hell with him, is destroyed.

It turned out that Pinhead's death had been much exaggerated. Just years later, that 2022 *Hellraiser* reboot was directed by David Bruckner, who went back to Barker's *The Hellbound Heart* for his version of Pinhead, focusing on the author's original description of the Cenobite: 'Its voice [. . .] was light and breathy – the voice of an excited girl. Every inch of its head had been tattooed with an intricate grid, and at every intersection of horizontal and vertical axis a jewelled pin driven through to the bone.' This seemed to give Bruckner an idea. Adding a little modern LGBTQ+ magic to the project, he told

Empire magazine that 'we liked the idea that the Cenobites had evolved beyond any kind of gender,' knowing he'd discovered his Pinhead the second he met trans actor Jamie Clayton. 'Jamie was so postured and controlled,' said Bruckner, 'and you got a sense of silky hunger underneath it all.'

The Barkerverse is infused with queerness, but how far does the author's own sexuality play a part in his fantastical genre-creating, world-building, monster-mashing work? Would Pinhead have existed in quite the same way if Barker himself was straight? Perhaps not: 'Being gay does provide an interesting tension,' he told *The San Francisco Examiner* in 1995. 'Part of me wants to say that I am just a regular guy, but another part of me says that there is a gay sensibility. This isn't just about acts performed in the bedroom – it alters your point of view, your aesthetic.'

JARETH THE GOBLIN KING

The babe with the power: David Bowie's queer-coded villain

'Those tights were a bit too tight, weren't they?' suggests actor Warwick Davis in *The Guardian* (2022). He is talking about the iconic outfit worn by his co-star David Bowie as goblin king Jareth in the beloved 1986 musical fantasy *Labyrinth*. With rock-star styling, bad-boy leather jackets, New Romantic frills, '[a] huge wig and seven pairs of socks down his tights', there's certainly something about Jareth.

Deliciously evil, camp and catty – and, according to the movie's makers, a teenage girl's idea of a rock-star boyfriend – it makes sense that many of us have a certain fondness for the goblin king. Of course, Bowie brings his own sense of theatrical queerness to the role; he was already known for his clever on-stage genderplay and for making purposefully confusing sexuality announcements (he told a reporter in 1972 he was gay, and another in 1976 he was bisexual, and later called himself a closet heterosexual). As he plays with his crystal balls, we are told the king's one true desire is *Labyrinth*'s female protagonist, Sarah, but it just doesn't feel authentic: there's clearly only one person Jareth has a sock-bulge for, and that's himself.

In this coming-of-age movie, Sarah – a precocious teenage Larper played by Jennifer Connolly in her first-ever role – flits around her local park dressed in fantasy garb, excitedly reciting her favourite book, *The Labyrinth*. Late to babysit her infant half-brother, Toby, and scolded by her (rather reasonable) stepmother, Sarah stomps angrily through the house. Toby won't stop crying and she pleads with the goblin king, the make-believe antagonist in her book, to just take him already. But then fiction becomes fact: Toby disappears from his cot and the king himself appears in a glittering black Maleficent-style onesie and impossibly huge back-combed wig – but, as the viewer can see, this is no regal goblin wrangler: it's crotch-bulging music icon David Bowie.

Labyrinth was always going to surprise. Directed by Muppet man Jim Henson, produced by *Star Wars* creator George Lucas, written (mostly) by Monty Python's Terry Jones, and full of Henson's wonderfully lumpy puppets, the movie has a truly unique sensibility. British artist Brian Froud's sketches were *Labyrinth*'s starting point – and not just for the characters themselves, but also for the costumes so brilliantly realized by fashion designer Ellis Flyte. 'The trickiest pieces were most of David's as they were designed to be highly original and didn't always transfer from sketch to actual garment!' said Flyte in an interview with Kent Hill in 2017. 'Plus we had a load of laughs with the stretch trousers over various codpieces.'

For fans who think Bowie's bulge is accidental: it was planned, discussed, and – at one point – shrunk down to a more conservative size. Henson and the others wanted Jareth to appear frightening to 15-year-old Sarah and made him an almost irresistible, wanton villain, using a codpiece to imply his raw sexuality. On The Jim Henson Company's YouTube channel, Jim's son Brian talks about how the studio were unhappy with its distracting size. On seeing the rushes, they apparently said, 'You're absolutely nuts if you think David's going to keep wearing that thing.' Brian Froud's son Toby – who, incidentally, plays infant Toby in the movie – also works in the film business as a conceptual designer. '[Jareth] is meant to be the sexual allure of everything,' he told *Huffpost* in 2016. 'Fairies and goblins in that whole realm [. . .] are meant to be tempting. He is meant to be a sexual icon, and the fact that he's a rockstar, that's why they chose someone like David Bowie to do it.'

It seems to be this unspoken sexuality that has lodged in the mind for so many fans who, having watched *Labyrinth* as kids, have grown up with Jareth's queer power. Forced to solve a seemingly endless labyrinth to save Toby, Sarah befriends all sorts of outsiders, creating a chosen family of sorts, who help and hinder her on the way. Eventually, she reaches Jareth's final temptation, a masquerade ball (is there anything camper?), where he glowers sexily in shimmer lipstick, his hair bigger than ever, and she starts to feel feelings. Many nervously joke that this Jareth-Bowie hybrid marked their own queer sexual awakening and the movie (and masquerade scene) sure does have its loyal fans. You can meet them at the Labyrinth Masquerade Ball, the almost-annual costume celebration in Los Angeles where side-characters Hoggle and Ambrosius can rub up against Jareth's goblins on the dancefloor. Otherwise, you might see Jareth himself on stage at drag extravaganzas, on TikTok in makeup tutorials, or on the arms of mega-fans (*Labyrinth* full-sleeve tattoos are a thing), or you can order a digitally printed copy of his pendant or a pair of 'Babe with the Power' earrings online.

At the end of the labyrinth, and the end of the movie, Sarah thwarts the goblin king, saves Toby and returns safely to her cutesy childhood bedroom. Everything is as it was; there are no more scary bulges or matted drag wigs, and normal life is restored – but for how long? Sarah has had a taste of the queer world and tonight Jareth will haunt her dreams.

MISS TRUNCHBULL

The butch, lesbian-coded big bad of Crunchem Hall

Beware of being nasty to a small, insignificant kid: you might just end up in their spellbinding children's novel, cult Hollywood adaptation, hit musical and adored reboot. The 'mean and loathsome' owner of a sweetshop frequented by hallowed author Roald Dahl as a young boy in Cardiff, Wales, served as inspiration for one of his most memorable villains, the loved, loathed and lesbian-coded Miss Trunchbull.

The antagonist from Dahl's novel *Matilda* (1988), the story of a cute telekinetic nerd disowned by her family, Miss Trunchbull is the sadistic, child-hating headmistress of Crunchem Hall who is still basking in the weakening glow of her sporting achievements. (She was a shot-putter, javelin-thrower and hammer-thrower, events that, in the movies, were performed at the 1972 Munich Olympics.) We know that Trunchbull, unlike Matilda's saviour, sweet yet downtrodden teacher Miss Honey, is a villain, not just by her words and actions but – as in most of Dahl's work – by her physicality: 'She was a gigantic holy terror, a fierce tyrannical monster,' writes the narrator, 'who frightened the life out of the pupils and teachers alike. There was an aura of menace about her even at a distance.' Her strength was otherworldly: 'looking at her, you got the feeling that this was someone who could bend iron bars and tear telephone directories in half.'

We get it: the Trunchbull is a villain, and a muscly one, too, but Dahl's novel and all the adaptations give her a strongly queer-coded countenance. She's unbelievably butch, oversized, sports-mad, loves a comfortable shoe, hates kids, asks, 'Why are all these women married?' and there's definitely no male love interest: all tired stereotyped attributes of queer women. Is Dahl's creation a villain because she's a lesbian?

'Sometimes these characters seem like warnings: *this* is what you'll be like if you choose a life outside of heterosexuality,' says author Daisy Jones to Sadhbh O'Sullivan in the latter's essay 'We Need to Talk about the Crazy Lesbian Trope' (Refinery29.com, 4 June 2021). The pair discuss how the 'butchness of *Matilda*'s unmarried (aka coded lesbian) Miss Trunchbull in contrast to Miss Honey is a prime example.' Although Trunchbull is not a canonically queer character, Jones and O'Sullivan think she might qualify for the Crazy

Lesbian trope, the concept of a woman so unhinged by same-sex desire that she is driven towards danger, destruction and criminal acts. And the notion that Trunchbull might share trope territory with Catherine Tramell, Sharon Stone's infamous crotch-flasher in *Basic Instinct* (1992), Natalie Portman's Nina in *Black Swan* (2010), or Jodie Comer's Villanelle in *Killing Eve* (2018), is delicious.

Matilda has always had its own LGBTQ+ fanbase, who find the film glowing with lesbian magic. The story of a young, bookish child who doesn't fit in is the starting point of almost every queer narrative and, at Crunchem Hall, Matilda certainly finds herself in a community of other outsiders. Ultimately, she liberates them all, banishes Trunchbull and saves her saviour, Miss Honey, and the two live happily ever after, embodying the very queer Chosen Family trope. But that's not the end of the story. If Daisy Jones and Sadhbh O'Sullivan are right, and butch Trunchbull is supposed to be a warning to women, then might *Matilda* use Miss Honey to show the 'good' way to be a woman (unlike Trunchbull, she is impossibly kind, loves children, loves floppy hats and gerberas, and dresses femme)?

Queer readers are having none of this and countless digital pages of femslash fan fiction offer a different perspective. They focus on the young, vivacious teacher as a lesbian, imagining her queer relationships with a museum curator or geeky bookseller, and share clips from the 1992 movie adaptation where Miss Honey (Embeth Davidtz) lowers her glasses. With Trunchbull, Honey and perhaps even the telekinetic child hero herself, is *Matilda* the original *L Word*?

Trunchbull is a satisfyingly horrible character to play. Those lucky enough to step into her incredibly comfortable shoes are Pam Ferris in Danny DeVito's cult 1996 movie (Ferris's performance is considered the OG version), Bertie Carvel on stage in Tim Minchin's musical adaptation and Emma Thompson in Minchin's slick 2022 reboot movie. In an interview in 2023, Thompson was asked on camera, somewhat confoundingly, which of her iconic characters 'would you love to see on a dating app and what would their bio say?' As quick as a shotput flung from a hairy, ham-like arm, Thompson said, 'Obviously Trunchbull. She'd be on Grindr,' the actor went on, perhaps misunderstanding that Grindr is primarily an app for gay men, although it is indeed a touchstone of queer culture, 'And I suppose her [bio] would say, "I mean it: don't even try anything."'

THE SANDERSON SISTERS
The Disney witches reawakened by queer magic

What makes a queer villain *iconic*? A little acidic campness, a pinch of outsider status? Teeth like tombstones, perhaps? Or is it a magical combination of all three? Enter the Sanderson sisters, Winnie, Mary and Sarah, a trio of 300-year-old snaggle-toothed witches from Salem, Massachusetts, and the unofficial queens of the Disney pantheon of queer-coded villains. Summoned by Max (a virgin) lighting a black candle, the sisters first appeared on our screens and in our nightmares in the summer of 1993 in the comic horror *Hocus Pocus*. At first, this Disney movie, starring Bette Midler, Sarah Jessica Parker and Kathy Najimy, was something of a dud and critics barely raised their eyebrows at what seemed to be an overplayed farce. Over the years, though, it has slowly earned itself generations of sweet young fans for whom it has become essential Halloween viewing. However, 'no one gags as hard for the film's trio of villains quite like the gays,' writes Breckon Hunter Wellborn at the online publication *Collider* (30 September 2022). And he's right.

The original *Hocus Pocus* just *feels* queer. There is nothing inherently LGBTQ+ about a storyline that deals in the accidental reawakening of three vampiric witches who need to absorb the lifeforce of innocent children to remain ever young, and yet 'its queerness is present in nearly every element', writes Kevin O'Keefe on Mic.com (30 October 2015). For instance, a stunningly odd set piece in which the Sanderson sisters distract party guests by storming the stage and performing a rendition of Screamin' Jay Hawkins's 'I Put a Spell on You' is pure drag poetry – and wonderfully superfluous to the plot. And it is true that each of *Hocus Pocus*'s stars, Bette, Sarah and Kathy, have a healthy queer fanbase – Bette from her *Beaches* and gay bathhouse singing days, Sarah from *Sex and the City* and *And Just Like That* . . . and Kathy from her star turns in the *Sister Act* movies and any number of comic TV guest roles. 'It's not a stretch to say that for many young adults, *Hocus Pocus* was their first introduction to Midler, a legend in her own right,' says O'Keefe. Was Disney aware of the queer pulling power of these three great shire horses of camp? Or was it happenstance?

'The Sanderson sisters, like the gays I know and love best, occupy most of their time by camping about and complaining about how youth is wasted on the young,' writes J Bryan Lowder (online magazine *Slate*, 31 October 2013), officially claiming *Hocus Pocus* as the Best Gay Halloween movie. 'It serves as an important bit of queer cinema,' echoes O'Keefe, unaware at that time of the sequel about to slither out of a darker realm, 'important in many ways because of the young audience it targets.' Although perhaps young LGBTQ+ people might hope for more sophisticated representation than three dentally challenged, child-killing hags. But then, with the warbled cry of, 'We're back, witches!' and 29 years after the first movie, *Hocus Pocus 2* manifested. If it could be argued that the original film is queer in subtext only, well, the sequel has gay culture front and centre. The filmmakers cleverly – and knowingly – acknowledged their LGBTQ+ fanbase and remixed the original tale in a cauldron full of queerness. Take the infamous 'I Put a Spell on You' scene from the original: in the sequel, the Sanderson sisters sing another impromptu number, only this time the set piece is subverted. Winnie, Sarah and Mary now find themselves mistaken for contestants in a Sanderson-sisters costume contest and battle a trio of drag queens (of course) – *RuPaul's Drag Race* girls Ginger Minj, Kahmora and Kornbread – for the crown. They bring the house down with a performance of Blondie's 'One Way or Another' at the Salem Scare Fest.

If you have ever been at a queer venue close to Halloween, you will have seen *Hocus Pocus*'s influence on drag close up. Midler's 'I Put a Spell on You' will be lip-synched with varying degrees of accuracy, wigs will be snatched, tricks will be tricked and the whole thing might just be a treat. When *Hocus Pocus 2* was released, drag queens who have spent their careers performing as the Sanderson sisters felt rather pleased with themselves. Miss Clair Voyance (who does a truly mean Winnie) told *Rolling Stone* in 2022 that 'Disney took a hint at who kept this movie alive, and who kept these characters alive for the past 30 years, which was the drag queens.' There are some at Disney who might just agree. Florida performer Nicole Halliwell, star of the long-running *It's Just A Bunch of Hocus Pocus: A Drag Tribute* show, was invited to the *Hocus Pocus 2* premier and rubbed witchy shoulders with Midler – with the drag star looking more like Winnie than Bette herself. Is it such a leap to think queer culture has helped keep the black flame of *Hocus Pocus* alive?

DARK WILLOW

The evil alter ego of Buffy's computer-coding witch

All hail Dark Willow, the ultimate lesbian avenger. Powered by primeval magic, black contact lenses and an 'I'm as mad as hell and I'm not going to take it any more' attitude, the teenage Goth witch from *Buffy the Vampire Slayer* was, for a brief moment in the glory days of late 1990s television, the queerest villain on our screens.

Dark Willow is an evil iteration of beloved long-term character Willow Rosenberg, played by Alyson Hannigan, the sweet Jewish computer nerd turned lesbian witch and vital member of Buffy's 'Scooby gang'. When she wasn't helping Buffy Summers (Sarah Michelle Geller) fight vampires, demons, or embodied evil, Willow would be in her teenage bedroom raising her grade-point average against a backdrop of plushies and the world's cutest pillowscape. In terms of lesbian acceptance, Willow was a landmark character. This was radical, queer representation in a prime-time show, and her slow evolution towards lesbian love – unthreatening, vanilla, softly risqué – arguably did more for LGBTQ+ youth than the It Gets Better campaign.

But love – and grief – do strange things. After the death of her shy girlfriend Tara (Amber Benson) in season six, the young witch finally snaps. At the time, the writers already had Willow battling an addiction to magic, cleverly eroding her too-perfect persona, and putting her in situations where her obsession endangered her friends. Her risky spells almost ended her relationship with Tara; the pair briefly split up but were reunited just before Tara's surprise death. Overtaken with anger, young Rosenberg opens her whole self to the power of magic, and Dark Willow soon emerges – sassy and sexy in equal measure – tantalizing Buffy's queer audience in previously unthinkable ways.

'Dark Willow is everything Willow is – a lesbian witch – and also evil and slutty, which is incredibly hot and also makes her gayer,' writes Rachel Kincaid in her '55 Fictional Witches, Ranked by Lesbianism' list (Autostraddle, 5 October 2018). Incidentally, Kincaid ranks Willow at number 3, Tara at number 2, and Dark Willow in the hallowed top spot. The witch's look changes to reflect her new nihilistic outlook and she goes from A-grade geek to dominatrix, with black hair, veined skin and those black, black eyes. 'It's like the baseline levels of gayness were refracted through a dark prism,' says Kincaid, 'to become something indescribably more potent.'

Buffy's fandom is unique, not just in its fervour and its enduring love of the landmark series, now more than 20 years old, but in the way it continues to fascinate academia. The critical essays, fan symposiums and rather serious lecture series that *Buffy* has spawned are impressive, revealing (or perhaps occasionally projecting) an incredible depth of meaning in interpretations of the characters' antics. In Cael M Keegan's essay 'Emptying the future: Queer melodramatics and negative utopia in *Buffy the Vampire Slayer*' (2016), Dark Willow soon apparates into view. Keegan points out that, although Willow's voyage into lesbianism is portrayed in a startling positive way, Dark Willow shows us another side. 'The negative potential of queerness to disassemble the social and reimagine the world itself, enacted through the conduit of Willow's darkening queer power, emerges as a dominant theme,' they write.

Towards the end of season six, in a swirl of crackling purple and green light, Dark Willow finds herself on a hilltop trying to destroy the world. Her friend Xander desperately tries to reason with her. Is this the 'negative potential of queerness' Keegan writes about, and can a little witchy lesbianism really have the potential to 'disassemble' the heteronormative world as we know it?

Pulitzer-nominated film critic Stephanie Zacharek is also a fan of the Slayerverse. In her piece 'Willow, Destroyer of Worlds' (*Salon*, 22 May 2022), which opens with a short verse from T S Eliot, she positions the show as comparable to Melville, Dickens and Flaubert: 'From the start "Buffy" has always had hidden, or not so hidden, strata of emotional riches. But now [. . .] "Buffy" has grown up and out into a deeply layered epic, with characters that some of us feel we know as well as Captain Ahab, David Copperfield or Emma Bovary.' At the time of writing, Zacharek was tracking those online message boards so integral to early *Buffy* fandom in order to pick up the vibe surrounding Tara's death and the birth of Dark Willow. Ahead of the season finale, she noted charges of *Buffy* being 'anti-gay, misogynist, or both'; and that, in killing off Tara, the show's creators had destroyed one of the few positive lesbian role models on television. So far, so fandom, but for Zacharek, the show ultimately redeemed itself in its finale scenes: 'Willow, far from being a cut-out angry lesbian, is more fleshed out, and more terrifyingly alive, than she has ever been before.'

In the end, only Xander – Willow's wisecracking best buddy since kindergarten – can quell the pain of the 'hopped up uber-witch' and save the world. He reaffirms their friendship, their intense platonic bond, and brings her back from the brink with unconditional queer acceptance and the words: 'I love scary, veiny Willow.' Her hair transforms from black back to red; Willow re-emerges and the pair collapse in each other's arms. World saved. *Buffy* marched on for another, final season; and, although Dark Willow was officially vanquished, Willow herself was never the same: her queerness was fully 'fleshed out' and – now and again – her eyes would flash darkly.

THE GIRL

The skateboarding Iranian queer vampire of Bad City

Welcome to Bad City, a lonely desert town where a mysterious shrouded vampire flits about in the shadows, a queer-edged bloodsucker who breaks all the rules of vampiric convention. In writer-director Ana Lily Amirpour's debut feature *A Girl Walks Home Alone at Night* (2014), the filmmaker swaps the Dracula cape for a chador, the ancient Transylvanian count for a skateboarding bi or ace young woman, the haunted castle for a dreamlike Iranian village, and the victim for the villain in the movie's eponymous 'Girl' played by Sheila Vand. Billed as the world's first Iranian vampire Western and highly stylized in widescreen black and white, *A Girl Walks Home . . .* is beloved by critics and horror fans, and a fresh spin on ancient magic. In Amirpour's movie, it's not just blood – rich, black and splattering – that the Girl has an insatiable taste for, but female vengeance. With her billowing chador fluttering like bat wings, she seeks out men who have wronged women.

Amirpour has resisted describing *A Girl Walks Home . . .* as a feminist text, and it is not an explicitly LGBTQ+ movie either, but its fans have detected more than a little queerness between the lines. Bad City is a patriarchal mess, and its women and queer inhabitants do all they can to survive. On the fringes of town, a drag queen known as Rockabilly (Reza Sixo Safai) dances with a balloon. 'If there's one political thing [in the movie], it's not the chador,' said Amirpour on the movie's release, 'it's Rockabilly, because it's not OK to be gay in Iran.' The Girl, as a vampire antihero, quietly terrorizes the streets with her own fanged brand of vigilante justice, and the men who fall foul to her ways are always worth the punishment, having abused or exploited women, especially sex workers like Atti (Mozhan Marnò).

Scenes of the Girl following men at night are themselves a delicious reversal of fortune; and the more nervous the men get, the more she seems to enjoy herself. A drug-dealing pimp with 'SEX' tattooed on his neck gets the end he deserves after picking up the Girl thinking she is on special offer (she bites off his finger before sucking his blood). Poor Atti seems to be next, only there is something tender between her and the Girl; they have an intense, queer-seeming connection. 'You're sad,' says the Girl. 'You don't remember what you want. You don't remember wanting. It passed long ago.' Atti's ability to feel desire has been extinguished by the men of Bad City, and the Girl just cannot take what little she has left. In the end, the Girl extinguishes both of the men who have harmed Atti and redistributes their wealth, handing their valuable baubles over to their victim.

Ultimately, the Girl's killing spree is complicated by Arash (Arash Marandi, aka the 'Persian James Dean'), who initially seems to be just the type to feature on the Girl's menu but reveals himself to be a good person. Will the Girl be able to keep her fangs out of him? They have their own tender moment, dancing in the Girl's bedroom to her 1980s vinyl collection (music stolen from her victims) under an iconic poster of Madonna (although, on closer inspection, it is Margaret Attwood; the writer gave permission to this almost-starring role in the movie). But their almost-romantic moment is just as integral and emotional to the movie as the Girl's night with Atti – is this ancient, chador-wearing vampire bisexual or asexual, like most coffin-sleepers seem to be?

'My love of vampires came from Anne Rice and, as a pre-teen, reading all the *Vampire Chronicles*,' Amirpour told StudioCanal, referencing the book series widely thought to drive a stake through the heart of heteronormativity (see page 116). 'A vampire is so many things: serial killer, a romantic, a historian, a drug addict,' she continued, 'they're sort of all these things in one.' In his review of the film, critic and broadcaster Mark Kermode agreed, describing the Girl as a shapeshifting presence (BBC Radio 2, 2014). One moment she's a young woman listening to music in her bedroom, another she's skateboarding in her chador like she's 'walked off the set of *Persepolis*,' he said; and in another moment she's a 'wraith lurking in the shadows in this way that harks back to Murnau's *Nosferatu* and *Bram Stoker's Dracula*.' (Kermode scored the move 5 out of 5.) Amirpour's Girl is both vampire and young woman, deathly menace and cute music-loving teen, bloodsucker, chador-wearing skater, bisexual and asexual. In this way, *A Girl Walks Home Alone at Night* brings together these wonky, incongruent and unexpected parts to make something wholly new with an undeniably queer, feminist vibe.

HARLEY QUINN

Our favourite chaotic, Jewish bisexual villain

Meet the Clown Princess of Crime, the chaotic bisexual Jewish antihero armed with killer one-liners, a brutal Brooklyn accent and a baseball bat and booby-trapped carnival mallet to smash away at heteronormativity. For more than two decades, Harley Quinn has backflipped through many iterations, from animated series to comics and video games to big-budget movies played perfectly by Margot Robbie. Although she might often be found on the arm of her 'puddin', Arkham's most evil henchman, the Joker, she might equally be found planting one on her sometime girlfriend, Poison Ivy.

Harley isn't a relic dusted off from an early DC comic; she first appeared in the debut season of *Batman: The Animated Series* in 1992. At the time, showrunners Paul Dini and Bruce Timm were looking for a female foil for the Joker or a gangster's moll love interest for Batman, but – POW! – they soon changed their minds when they saw comedian, screenwriter and actor Arleen Sorkin's comic turn dressed as a harlequin on *Days of Our Lives* (1991): they needed to think big! Arleen and Paul were college friends and, together, they worked out how they might they incorporate Sorkin into the DC family. Harley Quinn was inspired directly by Sorkin: her accent, mannerisms and comic outlook were all incorporated. 'Through Dini's transformation,' writes Alex Jaffe over at DC.com (2021), 'Arleen's witty, cabaret antics formed the meat and bones of what would become the media juggernaut we know today as Harley Quinn.' It makes sense that – just like Arkin – Harley has a little Jewish magic. 'As early as [the character's debut episode] "Joker's Favor", Harley can be heard lamenting her capture by Batman with a signature Yiddish "Oy." When she wants to impress the Joker in "Harley & Ivy", she remarks how he's gonna "plotz" – another Yiddish phrase, meaning to fall over or burst,' says Jaffe.

But what about her queer magic? Harley – like all DC characters – was rebooted in 2011 and again in 2016, slipping over to the DC Extended Universe and popping up in the live-action *Suicide Squad*, played by Margot Robbie with full Sorkin comic charm. There are some delicious one-liners: when Harley is introduced to Katana, a swordstress whose blade can trap the souls of her victims, she says, 'Love your perfume. What is that, the scent of death?' Then, things just get queerer and queerer. In 2017, after more than two decades of 'Is she/ isn't she?' the Clown Princess finally had her first canonical lesbian kiss in comic *Harley Quinn* #25 with co-conspirator Poison Ivy, another Dini creation. Fans of the characters had been shipping the pair since the late 1990s, and that same kiss was finally realized on screen in the animated adult series *Harley Quinn* in 2020. Harley had finally graduated from a kids' Batman cartoon to a place where the natural progression of her relationship with Poison Ivy could be as queer as can be.

That same year saw the release of Robbie's *Birds of Prey (and the Fantabulous Emancipation of One Harley Quinn)*, Harley's first solo live-action movie. Some queer fans were disappointed, claiming that Harley's bisexuality wasn't explicitly explored; but it is there, albeit in a series of girl gang one-liners, second glances and knowing smiles. Over the movie's intro, Harley says she's had her 'heart broken by both men and women' and she is clearly drawn to Jurnee Smollett's Black Canary, the gorgeous cabaret singer who can (almost) out-quip Quinn. But it's Mary Elizabeth Winstead's character that gives Harley the fizziest knickers: 'She calls herself Huntress. Fucking fabulous if you ask me,' froths Quinn, who spends the movie hanging off Winstead's every word, stopping mid-fight to breathlessly say, 'You are so cool,' and utterly melts when Huntress screeches

up on a motorbike, looking devastatingly dykey, flicking up her visor to say, 'Need a ride?'

Perhaps Margot Robbie's Harley will never return to our screens, but queer fans of the animated series continue to chart her relationship with Poison Ivy. In 2023, with the animated *Harley Quinn* in its third season, the super-gay romance where Harley and Ivy refer to each other as 'life partners' shows no sign of losing its KER-POW! energy. Sadly, Arleen Sorkin passed away in 2023, but without her talent and charisma, one of DC's most important and influential queer, Jewish and mirthful characters would never have existed.

ELI

Sweden's most infamous gender-nonconforming night monster

John Ajvide Lindqvist's 2004 novel *Let the Right One In* is beloved by horror fans everywhere, but it was its (first) movie adaptation in 2008 that made this nonbinary vampire–mortal love story into an international phenomenon. It now spans two movies (the original, and a rather good 2010 English-language remake, *Let Me In*, with Chloë Grace Moretz as Eli, now called Abby, and Kodi Smit-McPhee as Oskar, now Owen); a 2022 Showtime TV series; *Let Me In: Crossroads*, the graphic novel; and a play. Lindqvist wrote the screenplay for the original movie, remixing his own novel, turning down the volume on the book's subplots and character histories and turning up the central love story: a childhood friendship, a bloody coming-of-age narrative and a tentative, to-the-death romance.

On a snowy 1980s Swedish housing estate, 12-year-old Oskar (Kåre Hedebrant) is trying to survive. His parents have split up, his mother is terribly sad, and he is subjected to a horrific campaign of violent and humiliating bullying by his classmates – and he has his own anger issues, dreaming of revenge. Eli, a 'girl' seemingly the same age (played by Lina Leandersson), moves in next door. Eli tells Oskar they cannot be friends; but, slowly, Eli is proved wrong. The pair become close, tapping cute Morse code messages through the walls of their adjoining bedrooms, and Eli encourages Oskar to stand up for himself. However, Eli is no girl but rather a centuries-old vampire trapped in the body of a child, hunted by a vampire killer and responsible for a series of gruesome murders, a suicide and more.

What is stunning about the movie adaptation is how sparing Lindqvist is with information outside of Eli and Oskar's relationship, and with Oskar's experience of being bullied; much is suggested but little is explained, making the viewer work hard to solve the puzzle. In this way, Lindqvist deliberately obscures Eli's sex and gender. All we know is that, although Eli reads as female, they ultimately tell Oskar they are 'not a girl'.

In one scene Oskar's eyes widen when he sees Eli's naked form and surgical scarring where their genitals might be – only he keeps his surprise to himself. In the novel, this scene has a backstory showing that Eli is male; but in the movie, the character has no gender, reaffirmed by the over-dubbing of Eli's voice by actor Elif Ceylan to make it more enigmatic. But what's clearly fascinating to Lindqvist is Oskar's readiness to offer Eli acceptance: he has already come to terms with his friend's vampirism and Eli's sex is of little importance to him. In one intimate moment, Oskar asks Eli to be his girlfriend. 'Oskar,' says Eli, knowing their friendship might be at risk if they tell the truth, 'I'm not a girl.' Eli braces for rejection but Oskar's response is immediate and heartfelt: 'Oh, but do you want to go steady or not?'

To queer matters further, the bullying that Oskar is subjected to feels like a well-trodden gay-teen trope. Also, Oskar's father is still around, and a short scene shows him living with another man. It's unclear whether Oskar's father is gay, and therefore the viewer cannot know what it might mean for Oskar to be 'going steady' with someone who is 'not a girl'. But the boy loves Eli, nonetheless.

In Lindqvist's Sweden, everyone is lonely, isolated and misunderstood, dwarfed by the immense brutalist housing blocks and snow-laden parklands – everyone except Eli and Oskar, that is, who, somehow, find each other. In the end, theirs is a love that spans gender, sexuality, humanity and centuries – is this a platonic friendship, the beginnings of a nonbinary pansexual relationship, or the most perfect vampire–human love affair since Bella and Edward? The movie leaves the question delightfully vague. 'It is impossible to say why we love something or someone,' writes Lindqvist in his novel *Little Star* (2010). 'We can come up with reasons if we have to, but the important part happens in the dark, beyond our control. We just know when it is there.'

THELMA

The telekinetic teenage lesbian bird-killer of Norway

Like so many other young queer people, Thelma is relieved to finally move to the big city. At university in Oslo, away from her small-town, small-minded family, she can truly be herself. Her parents are too controlling, too religious, and have ill-prepared their daughter for the real world. But uptight 20-year-old Thelma is lonely, she has developed feelings for her friend, Anja, and is trying to navigate her sexuality from the depths of shame, embarrassment and guilt. So far, so gay. But imagine accepting your burgeoning lesbian powers only to discover you have uncontrollable, potentially murderous psychokinetic powers too?

In Joachim Trier's *Thelma* (2017), the Academy Award-nominated Norwegian supernatural thriller, the titular character played by Eili Harboe must overcome her gay shame, tame the monster within, forgive herself for past mistakes and enact a little well-deserved revenge while she's at it. But with mysterious seizures, flashes of painful hidden memories and nightmarish (and, let's face it, kind of erotic) visions of serpents, Trier gives Thelma the worst freshers' week ever.

All it takes is for Anja (Kaya Wilkins) to sit next to Thelma in the university library for the seizures to start, an orgasmic trigger that causes a flock of birds to dash themselves against the windows. Later, as she undergoes a brain test in a bunker-like hospital suite, she thinks again of Anja. 'Lord, save me from these thoughts,' she pleads, wishing that Anja, and her feelings for her, would disappear. And that's just what happens.

'The coming-out experience of *Thelma* is true to life in many ways,' writes Ciara Pitts in her article 'Welcome to the Rebirth of Lesbian Horror Movies' for *i-D* (7 September 2018). 'All the lead character wants is to live authentically, but the trepidation attached to that has become too overwhelming, making her believe that she's worthless.' Devastated by Anja's disappearance, Thelma starts to remember things from the past. Just why are her parents so wary of her? And she is an only child, so who is the mysterious little brother she sees in her dreams? The movie poses the question: will Thelma forever be a queer villain, or can she unpick this unholy mess, bring back Anja and ultimately redeem herself? What's a young psychokinetic lesbian to do?

Thelma might have her human antagonists (her parents, those classic mean girls), but the real monster she must fight is her sense of internalized homophobia. For the director, this all stems from ancient dogma. In 2017, Trier said to Mic.com's Corey Atad that, 'If I am being critical of something, it's how religion can be used as a power structure, a function to suppress, and historically, particularly [suppress] women or people who are gay.' And so, the true villain in Trier's lesbian horror movie is the overbearing conservatism of religion, the effects of sexual repression and the idea of female sexuality as an unfathomable power that cannot be stymied or controlled. Are Thelma's religious parents trying to shame her natural psychokinetic powers into submission, or is it her queerness – or both?

Writing in 2018 on the release of queer cabin-in-the-woods lesbian horror *What Keeps You Alive*, Pitts hoped both movies might signal a much-needed update to the genre. For decades, lesbian horror would end with a nihilistic trope like Bury Your Gays or Lesbian Tragedy, but not *Thelma* or *What Keeps You Alive*. Both stories 'transcend stereotypes,' says Pitts, and 'Trier [. . .] beautifully convey[s] the horrors that lie within the minds of the marginalised, creating chillingly accurate metaphors that assure us we're not alone.' Although not as hopeful as Pitts, writer Rachel Kincaid seems to agree: 'Gay women, of course, are used to watching movies with lesbians and hoping against hope that they'll end up safe and happy; that they'll at least live,' she writes (Autostraddle, 31 October 2018). 'Horror featuring lesbians is an interesting gamble in that it asks straight viewers [to] feel the same way, that they'll root for our survival.'

Along Thelma's path to lesbian redemption are some clever reveals that make the viewer question her victimhood. Unable to control her powers, the danger of imminent death is constant; but there is a delightfully unexpected aspect to *Thelma*. Although she certainly has her villainous moments (her vengeful rage fries one character to a crisp), she ultimately defies our expectations, psychokinetically escaping the confines of the genre, and finally gets the girl.

THE BABADOOK
The nightmarish outsider haunting queer memes

It is Jennifer Kent we can thank for unleashing the Babadook onto the world. The Australian film director cast him as the main character in her 2014 psychological horror *The Babadook*. Here he plays the physical embodiment of a child's endless grief, a monster rendered in scratchy edges with long, child-catcher fingers, a truly horrifying manicure and questionable style choices that include a comical top hat. Amelia is the exhausted and isolated mother of Samuel, a cute but slightly creepy six-year-old who becomes convinced that the Babadook, a mildly threatening children's book character, is real. Things soon start to go bump in the night, Sam's behaviour becomes more erratic, and a mystery forms: is the 'Dook just the fantastical night terror of a child, a symbol of the damaged psyche of a young mother, or is he a demonic presence out to destroy the family? The movie was well-received on its release and soon gained an outsized international fanbase thrilled with Kent's cerebral approach to horror. But there was one audience demographic that – for some reason – seemed to love the Babadook more than any other. Apropos of nothing, Kent's shadowy, nightmarish monster earned himself a slew of LGBTQ+ fans, and soon the Babadook was a queer icon.

In 2017, when *The Babadook* relaunched on Netflix, a meme tsunami swept the internet, flooding it with shonky images that dropped Baba into queer or camp situations – from *RuPaul's Drag Race* to Baba at Pride wearing a T-shirt that reads 'Prepare to be Babashook' to Baba spotted on stage as the next guest star in *Chicago*, to a scrapbooking class, and even accepting an award from Human Rights Campaign. The inciting incident is as shadowy as the Babadook himself. Legend has it that a Netflix employee misfiled the movie, accidentally adding it to the streamer's LGBTQ+ selection – although there is no evidence to suggest this is true. But, with any meme-based moment, discovering its initial spark is near meaningless. The Babadook had become an unlikely star in the queer digital subculture, and that's that.

Once you see the 'Dook as queer, it's hard to see him as anything but. When the Babadook first enters Amelia and Sam's life, he is a mere character in a seemingly harmless children's book. 'The grieving widow of Kent's film discovers him in a frightening, flamboyant pop-up book on her son's shelf,' writes Eren Orbey in *The New Yorker* (17 June 2017). 'Fearing the creature's transgressive influence – his shameless oddity, his aggressive manner – she attempts to burn his manifesto, only to learn that attempting to get rid of the Babadook actually enlivens him.' And still, the monster's influence grows. In a time of contemporary book bans and burnings – from too-queer titles to titles apparently not queer enough – Amelia's attempts at purging her home of Babadookness seem, well, like well-trodden queer territory. At the end of Kent's movie, Amelia hasn't quite defeated the Babadook but instead learns to live with him in begrudging acceptance, something many LGBTQ+ people have experienced in their own families.

Much has been made of *The Babadook*'s exploration of the unachievable and ultimately misogynistic expectations we put on mothers. How the movie deals with trauma, showing how it can haunt us like a demon, pushes Amelia to the very limit of sanity. Again, queer audiences can relate: stress and isolation can feel maddening and hiding your true self can feel like there's a monster inside, clawing its way out. Orbey goes further than most in solving the mystery of the Babadook's queer villainy. He notes that the movie's preoccupation with trauma and loss might have something to do with it. 'The gay community, witness to so many horrors, is expert at mining spunk and solidarity from what might otherwise seem only tragic,' he says.

MADAME BLANC

Dario Argento's lesbian witch reimagined by queer-edged Tilda Swinton

It is 1977, the Baader–Meinhof gang has terrified West Berlin with bombings and assassinations and the city has plunged into existential peril. And yet Luca Guadagnino's *Suspiria* (2018) feels separated from time and space; there is just the constant rain, grey skies darkening and a queasy atmosphere that infects everything. This is the starting point of the Italian director's reimagining of Dario Argento's 1977 cult horror movie, but the Berlin grey soon gives way to bright colour; there's a bloodbath to come. And at the centre of it all is a rather queer mystery powered by the enigmatic Madame Blanc, artistic director and choreographer of a prestigious German dance academy, itself a front for a coven of witches. With its sexual awakenings, leggings and leotards, strict all-female boarding-school setting, witchcraft and devilry, mean-girl power grabs and an almost all-woman cast, *Suspiria* couldn't have more lesbian potential if it tried.

Guadagnino beamed his favourite collaborator into the lead role, and actor Tilda Swinton gives Blanc her best chain-smoking sapphic-witch-just-trying-to-keep-it-all-together energy. Throughout the movie, Blanc is buffeted by the coven's power struggles, but with Dakota Johnson's Susie, the innocent American dance student who joins her dance company, she remains serene. She mentors Susie, helping her to connect with her inner creative voice, and soon the young ingenue spills Blanc her sexiest secrets. After a particularly intense, near-orgasmic dance rehearsal, and over some chicken wings, Blanc asks Susie 'how it felt inside' and her reply comes as a shock: 'Like what it must feel like to fuck.' Madame Blanc is fascinated.

Suspiria, in all its intense eroticism, holds back from putting sex on screen. All the movie's queer sexuality is in the dance studio, with its writhing, almost-naked women's bodies, and coded into the costumes. What seems on Blanc's nightgown to be a tulip print is, in close-up, a series of contorted women. Sara (Mia Goth) sleeps in a cute pyjama set with tiny flowers that are actually breasts; and Miss Vendegast's (Ingrid Caven) blouse features roses that look like vulvas. The coven also wears archive Halston and Missoni pieces, making them the most stylish queer dance-witches in modern cinema.

Under Blanc's tutorship, Susie soon rises to the top of the troupe and performs in the star spot at the academy's startlingly creepy 'Volk' dance. But Blanc has other plans for Susie – and not just the lunging-in-a-leotard kind. At the beginning of the movie, a student (played by Chloë Grace Moretz) confides in sympathetic local psychotherapist Dr Josef Klemperer; she's terrified and hints at trouble at the academy. In Madame Blanc's hands, Susie is clearly in grave danger. 'No lie,' Johnson said to *Elle* magazine in 2018, '[the movie] fucked me up so much that I had to go to therapy.'

After their orgasmic dance and chicken-wing turning point, Swinton's Blanc becomes obsessed with Susie, training her and readying the young student for the upcoming dance performance and the complex witchy occult rituals that Madame Blanc needs her to perform. Soon, Tilda is in Susie's head, invading her dreams, while vulva-shaped light projections dance around her. And then the bloodbath: at the film's climax, Blanc seems to lose control and her student turns out to be more powerful than any of them could imagine.

Casting Tilda as Blanc (and, curiously, two other characters in the movie, male and female, her identity hidden behind prosthetics) brings its own queerness to *Suspiria*. From having been muse to gay filmmaker Derek Jarman in the mid-1980s, through to playing Virginia Woolf's gender-bending Orlando in Sally Potter's beloved 1990s movie and a gender-queer angel in *Constantine* (2005), there is certainly a through-line to

Swinton's career. In 2021 she gave a pleasingly left-field interview to gay playwright Jeremy O Harris for *British Vogue*, confusing everyone with her unique understanding of the Q word. 'I'm very clear that queer is actually, for me anyway, to do with sensibility,' she said, 'and finding that shared sensibility in others, like Guadagnino, is like finding family [. . .] I always felt I was queer,' she went on. 'I was just looking for my queer circus, and I found it.'

GINGER FITZGERALD
The queer teenage werewolf who just won't take it any more

The year 2000 was dominated by big-budget dude movies like *X-Men*, *The Patriot*, *The Perfect Storm*, *Gladiator*, the second *Mission: Impossible* movie and even *Nutty Professor II: The Klumps*. With each release proudly failing the Bechdel test and dripping with testosterone, by the end of the summer most moviegoers would have grown chest hair. But then along came *Ginger Snaps*, the little Canadian movie that couldn't have been more transgressive. The scrappy teen-wolf horror was the perfect antidote to all that glossy male saviourism with its two death-obsessed sisters, Ginger and Brigitte Fitzgerald, puberty woes, period panties and an underlying werewolf queerness trying to claw its way out.

In *Ginger Snaps*, a pair of grumpy Goth-edged sisters in suburban Ontario make a pact to leave their small town by the age of 16 – or to die trying. One night, as Ginger (Katharine

Isabelle) suddenly gets her first period, the scent of blood draws a mysterious creature and the sisters barely survive an attack in which Ginger is bitten. Soon, her body starts to change, hair begins to grow and Brigitte (Emily Perkins) watches on as her sister becomes aggressive and deliciously wanton; she has been bitten by a werewolf. Linking the menstrual cycle to werewolf lore seemed obvious and yet no one had done it before. Being a werewolf gives Ginger the excuse to act out her inner desires without restraint. She feels horny, she has sex; she feels like hurting her enemies, she does just that. And if she has the bloodlust to murder someone? Well, you can see where this is going. The tagline of the movie was 'They don't call it the Curse for nothing'.

If centring the story of two teenage female protagonists felt brave, a shot of Ginger's bloody panties in the first reel was taboo-breaking. So many horror filmmakers create for an imagined young male audience, but writer Karen Walton and director John Fawcett didn't care about all that. They knew they were making a lo-fi, feminist work, periods and all. So, how did the horror bros cope? 'When it first came out, no one fucking watched it,' said actor Katharine Isabelle to *Den of Geek* in 2020. But then something interesting happened. *Snaps* was released on VHS and, by word of mouth, it slowly spread like a werewolf virus. 'Emily [Perkins] and I thought we'd be the only people that liked it because we were weird and dark. We had no idea that through the generations it would continue to have an effect on people.'

Queer ideas surrounding *Ginger Snaps* have bubbled away since 2000, with culture writers forever enamoured with the movie's refreshing take on bloody teenage womanhood, puberty and unbridled feminist energy. But the relationship between Ginger and Brigitte, ostensibly sisters, deserves some unpacking. A close analysis by writer Noah Berlatsky uncovers the movie's LGBTQ+ themes as he gnaws at the bond between the girls. To him (and many others online), it looks less like sisterly affection and more like queer desire. In 'Sister Lovers: the Curse of Queerness in *Ginger Snaps*' (*WeAreTheMutants*, 8 October 2020), Berlatsky points out inconsistencies in how the sisters are presented: the girls look unrelated (the boys in the movie comment on this), they're in the same year and class at school, and, 'in a queasy scene towards the film's end, Ginger, more than half-transformed into wolf, leans into Brigitte and husks, "We're almost not even related any more." ' He wonders aloud why the pair are so alienated from their peers. 'But if you accept what you're actually seeing,' he claims, 'then the dynamic is obvious. Two girls who really are not sisters are engaged in a passionate, intense, open same-sex relationship. Their peers hate them for it.'

The idea that Ginger and Emily can be read as queer relies, in part, on how they break with gender convention. 'It was important that the power balance shifted,' said John Fawcett to *The Guardian* in 2021, 'and Ginger became "the alpha male". That's why when she attacks her classmate Jason, she shouts: "Who's the fucking guy now?" ' Berlatsky points out that this 'chaotic confusion' surrounding gender could be 'a metaphor for trans experience, for lesbian experience, for male gay experience.' What's more, throughout *Snaps*, Brigitte and Ginger try to conceal Ginger's werewolf identity; her true self must be closeted at all costs – a queer trope if ever there was one.

But, to Isabelle, *Ginger Snaps*' take on gender is the movie's true message. 'I think the film's legacy,' she said to *The Guardian* in 2021, more than two decades after the movie's release, 'is in how it takes the teenage female experience so seriously in a world where it's constantly disregarded.' Those lucky enough to discover *Snaps* during that summer of jacked-up, man-focused movies might have had their own sense of gender thoroughly queered with the movie's charming comic horror. 'My favourite line,' said Isabelle, 'is when I say to Brigitte: "I can't have a hairy chest, B, that's fucked!" The dark humour will never age.'

JENNIFER CHECK
Megan Fox's transgressive demonic succubus

To understand bisexual comic-horror masterpiece *Jennifer's Body*, you must first understand the mystery that is Megan Fox. In 2009 in Los Angeles, the actor was a world away from her strict religious upbringing in Tennessee and her isolating middle-school years (during which she was bullied) and was perhaps at the height of her fame. Although she had already picked up several small movie roles and a sitcom, it was Michael Bay's mega-budget *Transformers* (2007), and an infamous scene where a barely dressed Fox is draped across a Camaro, that positioned her as a sex symbol.

Fox scored countless cover shoots with men's mags and 'hottest' whatever awards, but with the attention came prudish criticism, accusations of artificiality and those misogynist noughties celeb-gossip sites that cravingly tracked the actor's weight, relationships, tattoos and Starbucks consumption. By

2009, as she starred in both *Transformers 2* and an endless marketing campaign that overexposed the movie and its stars, Fox became desired and detested in equal measure. But this was also the year of *Jennifer's Body*, the surprising indie movie by screenwriter Diabolo Cody that co-starred Amanda Seyfried, a gloriously messy take-down of high-school politics, female teenage-hood relationships, mediocre boys and the man-eater myth.

The story focuses on Anita 'Needy' Lesnicki (Seyfried), the downtrodden teenage frump to Fox's beautiful but mean Jennifer, a popular girl Needy idolizes. One night, Jennifer takes Needy to see a band at a local bar. Needy is thrilled but a fire breaks out; and in the aftermath, Jen is led away into the woods by the all-male band. Later that night, when she turns up at Needy's house, something has changed. Jennifer has been transformed into a sexy demonic succubus and spends the rest of the movie devouring boys, with Needy trying to stop her.

Casting Fox as Jennifer was a masterstroke. The *Transformers* star was already thought of as a man-eater, and Jennifer's attempts to hide her real self – i.e., demonic disemboweller – played into Fox's own perceived dualism and those misogynistic accusations of being artificial. But didn't all that hiding one's true identity seem kind of queer, too? And what of Needy's obvious crush on Jennifer and her body, and the tangled, confused sexual energy between the pair? Cody's script, with direction from Karyn Kusama, turned *Jennifer's Body*'s queerness up to 11, underlining the very LGBTQ+ pain and humour of being in love with your best friend. The filmmakers make this clear in the first reel: Needy's adorably unhinged narration describes how perfect Jennifer is as she first wafts on to the screen, until a classmate's voice telling her she's 'totally lesbi-gay' breaks her out of her reverie. But it's too late: the queer tone is set – as is Needy's role as the movie's chaotic bottom.

With Jennifer on the rampage and bodies piling up, Needy must step up and kill not just her beloved crush but her demonic BFF. The final blood-soaked showdown between Jennifer and Needy is as queer as anything and thrillingly sexy, with a passionate kiss, a bite and Needy – knife in hand – breathlessly straddling Jennifer's body.

Just like Michael Bay, Cody and Kusama focus on Fox's physical form; the camera tracks Jennifer's body swimming naked in the still black waters of a lake, her wet tongue as she flicks it through a flame, her toned abs in those tiny, cropped hoodies (it's 2009; there's a lot of midriff). But if Bay knowingly used the comforting cliché of hot-girl-hot-wheels to create a sexualized image of Fox in *Transformers*, Cody and Kusama took the actor's perfect form and queered her, giving her demon teeth and reptile eyes and splattering her with deathly black vomit.

So, why was *Jennifer's Body*, now celebrated as a gory feminist marvel, a flop on release? Fox was at the height of her powers, Seyfried had starred in *Mean Girls* in 2004 and Diabolo Cody had just made the hugely popular *Juno* (2007); it just didn't make sense. With hindsight, the movie's new fanbase suspects marketing was something to do with it. The trailer gave audiences the impression that *Jennifer's Body* was a sexy lesbian romp, whereas the movie is anything but – leaving everyone disappointed. As Carmen Maria Machado writes in *It Came From the Closet: Queer Reflections on Horror* (2022), this had critics writing the movie off as 'queerbaiting, gay for titillation, performatively lesbian' – and Machado could hardly blame them as 'the film was marketed in precisely this fashion, highlighting Megan Fox's tongue dipping into Amanda Seyfried's mouth.' Nevertheless, *Jennifer's Body* started to gain an audience; perhaps the Me Too reckoning of 2017–18 helped re-evaluate what the press had done to Fox and gave us a little of what we needed: to see male misogynists chewed up and spat out.

Machado, a fan of the movie, is most fascinated by the complicated subtext: 'one of the most interesting things about this film,' she says, 'is that it is not a film about lesbians, per se.'

Instead, Machado is drawn to the movie's take on how all of us, as teens, navigate our inner desires whatever they may be. '[*Jennifer's Body*'s] energy is exceptionally specific: what it means to experience parallel sexualities with your best friend as you punch through the last vestiges of childhood; and, significantly, the central body of water that is bisexuality.'

There may be another reason why fans have started to look again at *Jennifer's Body*. In 2010, just one year after the movie was released and years before it 'broke through', Megan Fox spoke to *Esquire* about her own bisexuality, and she's been outspoken about it ever since (in 2021, during Pride month, she reminded us all in a humble Instagram post that she's been 'Putting the B in #LGBTQIA for over two decades'). Of course, in most situations the sexuality of an actor shouldn't matter, but *Jennifer's Body* had already been so clever with its casting; perhaps it was a little prescient, too? 'I thought you only murdered boys,' says Needy in one scene. At which Jennifer smiles and reminds her, 'I go both ways.'

URSULA THE SEA WITCH

The ultimate Disney villain with true queer heritage

Tentacled supervillain Ursula the Sea Witch is perhaps Disney's queerest character. A rambunctious, gravel-voiced Cecaelia, the human-octopus hybrid of contemporary mythology, she strikes deals with miserable merfolk to make their dreams come true – and more besides. In Disney's animated classic *The Little Mermaid* (1989), young mer-teen Ariel is one of Ursula's 'Poor Unfortunate Souls' for whom the sea witch conjures a pair of human legs so she might pursue love on land – only she snatches away Ariel's voice while she's at it. Ursula is larger than life, all knowing winks with turquoise eyeshadow, rouge lips and a kilowatt smile. She's theatrical, flawless, and clearly drag-inspired.

In the mid-1980s, there was something fishy going on at Disney. The studio had been working on an adaptation of the iconic Hans Christian Andersen fairytale *The Little Mermaid*, but it needed a creative who would bring their everything to the project. They were looking for an auteur who could produce, write songs and breathe life into the movie and its characters. Howard Ashman was the young playwright whose off-Broadway musical *Little Shop of Horrors* was not only a hit, but was also being made into a movie by Frank Oz. Disney took a meeting with the boy from Baltimore.

'He was uniquely suited to the job,' write Nicole Pasulka and Brian Ferree in culture magazine *Hazlitt* (14 January 2016). 'Like so many creative people who'd grown up in Baltimore during the 1950s and 1960s, the intersection of raunchy drag queens and fairytales was Howard Ashman's sweet spot.' And so, Ashman reached for another Baltimore boy, one of the city's most legendary performers, to inspire *The Little Mermaid*'s most villainous character, Ursula. Previously unleashed by 'Pope of Filth' John Waters in his movie *Roman Candles* (1966) was Harris Glenn Milstead, also known as drag queen Divine.

Milstead had spent most of his childhood in Lutherville, Maryland, then a lip-bitingly boring and conservative American suburb. Plump and feminine, Milstead was bullied, but finally found kinship with his neighbour, amateur filmmaker Waters. It was Waters who encouraged his new friend to develop his drag alter ego, and Divine was born.

Ashman's upbringing was like Milstead's, but he had one thing the drag monster hadn't: youth theatre. Both Ashman and his young sister were delightful show-offs, but it was Howard who went from the Baltimore Children's Theater Association to college and then to New York City, with his boyfriend Stuart White in 1974, to write and direct theatre. He wrote plays, White helped restore the old WPA Theater, and both immersed themselves in the queer performance scene. Ashman's musical *Little Shop of Horrors* was a hit, but White died in 1983, soon after opening, a victim of the AIDS epidemic.

In his grief, Ashman still managed to electrify the production of *Mermaid*, bringing his own Broadway sensibilities to the role and hiring a slew of theatre names who found him utterly inspirational. Ursula was voiced by veteran stage actor Pat Carroll, who during rehearsals asked Ashman to sing Ursula's big song, 'Poor Unfortunate Souls'. 'Well, he put on the cloak, sang the song; he was brilliant,' she said in *Treasures Untold: The Making of The Little Mermaid* (2006), 'I watched everything, I watched his face, I watched his hands; I ate him up!'

The movie – and Ursula – were a hit and Ashman seems to have been embraced by Hollywood, becoming part of the Disney Renaissance, writing on *Aladdin* and helping make *Beauty and the Beast* into a musical. But those mermaid waters

were dark and deep. Ashman was a gay man in conservative, anti-gay Reagan-era America, working at the height of the AIDS epidemic, and had just seen his partner die of the disease. Perhaps all this adds a sense of urgency to Ursula's queerness? Ashman's sea witch doesn't play by the rules. She may be thought of as the villain but she's certainly having all the fun. Through Ashman, Disney had something truly subversive in Ursula: she was liberated and liberating, and she became one of the most iconic animated characters of Disney's output. Was this what Hans Christian Andersen had imagined for his little mermaid? Probably not. But Ursula sparkles darkly on screen.

Ashman discovered he was HIV positive in 1988 during production of *The Little Mermaid*. Disney put together a production studio near Ashman's home so he could attend hospital visits in NYC, but at that time there had been almost 21,000 deaths from AIDS in the US and contemporary treatment solutions were years away. He died in 1991, leaving behind a legacy of iconic characters – and delightfully twisted camp ones, too – from Audrey II in *Little Shop of Horrors* to the Divine drag-inspired Ursula in *The Little Mermaid*. That same year, *Beauty and the Beast* was released with a special dedication: 'To our friend Howard, who gave a mermaid her voice, and a beast his soul. We will be forever grateful.'

NANCY DOWN

The world's most notorious, best-dressed Goth witch

'I bind you, Nancy, from doing harm,' murmurs Sarah. 'Harm against yourself and harm against other people.' But her spell doesn't do much at all and the Nancy in question – the queerest, coolest Goth-witch the world has ever known – flies through the air screaming, dagger in hand, unhinged and unbound. Welcome to the world of *The Craft*, the beloved 1996 teen movie that – more than 25 years later – continues to have a spellbinding impact on style, Halloween costumes, Etsy merch and a generation of queer witches.

In 1990s Los Angeles, troubled new student Sarah meets a group of girls at St Benedict's Catholic school. The three punk-edged outcasts are trauma survivors, called witches by other students, and look utterly incredible. Rochelle, played by Rachel True, is the victim of racist bullies; shy Bonnie, played by *Party of Five* actor Neve Campbell, hides her horrific scars from a car accident, and Nancy, the loud-mouthed villain of the piece, played by *Return to Oz* child star Fairuza Balk, lives in near poverty with her mother and abusive stepfather. They befriend Sarah and, eventually, tell her about Manon, a spirit they worship in their witchy after-school meetups. But with Sarah now part of the coven, the girls' fun-but-faux magic becomes supercharged and, as a surprise to them all, their spells start to work. They soon become masters at 'the craft', charming butterflies and levitating at slumber parties, and enact delicious revenge on their bullies. But power does strange things to the group dynamic, petty jealousies abound and Nancy reveals herself to be the movie's true antagonist – and one of the most memorable messed-up characters in pop culture.

It would be easy to underestimate the influence of *The Craft*. Generations of teenagers find themselves entranced by the movie, its 1990s music and fashion references continue to excite, and it has helped power a woo-woo fascination with crystals, smudge sticks and tarot (interestingly, a real-life Wiccan, Pat Devin, was the film's on-set advisor). But its popularity with queer women is astonishing. Perhaps it is because *The Craft* feels feminist in approach; fascination with magic and the occult tends to be more of a female and queer-adjacent domain. Or is the movie's popularity with LGBTQ+ people because Nancy is, quite simply, a total badass?

It might be more than enough for queer *Craft* lovers to view the movie through its subtext, but there are moments where Nancy's character brings lesbian desire very much into the conversation – usually diffused by her trademark coarse humour. In an early scene, a butch female security guard, clearly lesbian coded, patrols the high-school halls and Nancy sarcastically suggests to the two other girls, 'Maybe she could be our fourth?' Rochelle and Bonnie laugh nervously and Nancy continues, emboldened: 'Come on, I love a woman in uniform!' It's a seconds-long moment but marks out Nancy, and *The Craft* itself, as sexually transgressive. Later, at a candlelit slumber party, Sarah asks the others if they have ever played the game Light as a Feather, Stiff as a Board. 'One girl lays down and you surround her? And you put your fingers underneath?' she says. 'Put your fingers where?' smirks Nancy, in another incredible outfit (spiked dog collar, PVC leggings and slicked-back hair), extending her hand to make the universal gesture of double-digit fingering. The girls all laugh and scoff, but moments later, the coven indeed 'fingers' Rochelle. They kneel around her lying body. 'Now, you take your index finger and middle finger,' instructs Sarah in a sexy drawl, 'and put it under her, like this,' and the trio slowly but magically levitate their friend. The scene is incredibly intimate, the girls' breathless awe is unlocked by physical touch, lesbian energy crackles through the air.

In 2020, *The Craft* earned itself a reboot. *The Craft: Legacy*, directed by Zoe Lister-Jones, was celebrated for its trans inclusion but was conspicuous for its straightness (there is one bisexual character, but he doesn't survive the final act). Didn't moviemakers know that it was queer women who kept the *Craft* brand alive? That said, perhaps a certified lesbian version of *The Craft* might quell some of its queer magic. In the simpler days of 1996, a glimmer in the subtext – rather than an officially LGBTQ+ master narrative – might just have made it a more desirable piece of pop culture for queer people.

But then there's Nancy. Easily the standout star of *The Craft*, Fairuza Balk's performance is magnetic. She gets the best outfits and the best dialogue, and exudes raw sexuality and unlimited power. It's little wonder she is something of a queer icon and queen of a thousand memes: she may be unhinged but she gets to say and do anything she likes. What queer person doesn't want to craft that?

CROWLEY

Fantasy icon Neil Gaiman's favourite fallen angel

It's the end of the world as we know it, heaven is about to crash into the Earth, hell is rising, and Neil Gaiman's fandom is fizzing with excitement. The British fantasy author's cult TV show *Good Omens* (2019), based on his beloved 1990 collaborative novel with Terry Pratchett, is a playful imagining of the End Times and the two fantastical creatures who try to stop it. Starring Satan's son, the Four Horsemen, Gabriel (Jon Hamm), Beelzebub (Anna Maxwell Martin) and other favourite characters from the biblical universe, *Good Omens'* real heroes are fussy angel Aziraphale, played by Welsh actor Michael Sheen, and his unlikely best friend, the villainous and sinuous demon Crowley, played by David Tennant. Over 6,000 years, the odd pair – both sort of celestial foreign diplomats – have grown to love the Earth and come together to sabotage Satan's big plans.

Gaiman was showrunner for *Good Omens* and his fingerprints are all over this delightful franchise, with its Brit-focused casting, clever dialogue and endless comic mishaps – a little like a supernatural *Four Weddings and a Funeral*. Another creator might have had Aziraphale and Crowley trying to clip each other's wings, but in *Omens* the pair grow fond of each other, share advice, offer support and hope to save the only place their friendship can endure. The performances of Sheen and Tennant, both great friends IRL, are spellbinding and hint at a more fleshed-out, closer connection between the characters, hidden from view. To anyone deeply invested in angel and demon lore, Aziraphale and Crowley seemed to be a queer couple, and it wasn't long before fans imagined a romantic connection between the pair.

Not everyone loved that first season. A misfiring Christian group in the US infamously organized a petition to 'tell Netflix to cancel blasphemous *Good Omens*' even though the show's platform is Amazon (which is a very *Good Omens* thing to do). But fans were frustrated too: why were show spokespeople describing this queer couple as just good friends? Didn't they know that *Omens* fans had been discussing the pair's mutual attraction since the 1990s? To make matters more complicated, Gaiman himself, who enjoys true dialogue with his fandom, was asked about it on X (then Twitter): 'So . . . they're gay, right?' He answered plainly: 'They're an angel and demon, not male humans.'

You can't blame the fans for their queer anticipation. Gaiman's work has always been LGBTQ+ friendly. His masterwork, *The Sandman*, debuted in 1988 as a startlingly modern comic and is the source material for some of the queerest movies and contemporary TV shows out there. 'When I was writing it – and today – I had gay friends and I had trans friends,' Gaiman told *The Queer Review* in 2022. 'I wanted to see them represented [. . .] and if I left them out, then I wouldn't be representing my world, or the world that I was in, or the world I was perceiving accurately, bravely, or truly. And that's the point of art.'

The press also picked up on the fandom's queer yearnings and asked Gaiman if he had considered making Aziraphale and Crowley's relationship canonically gay. Again, he pointed out that, in the world of *Omens*, 'Angels are sexless unless they specifically make an effort,' quoting the original novel. But the fandom, often a few steps ahead of their creator, thought Gaiman and the show makers doth protest too much. Look at Aziraphale's Victorian dandy outfits, they said! His peroxide hair, his fussiness (unfortunately almost always a shorthand for gay)! And what about Crowley's joyous femme looks? Just who was Gaiman trying to kid? To the fandom, the pair were lovers, a gay couple, or a trans allegory, celebrated in fan art and eroticized in some incredibly steamy fan fiction.

And then – four years later – came season two, and fans, critics, heavenly beings and just about everyone else accepted that *Good Omens* has a queer love story at its heart. It might not have been Aziraphale and Crowley's romance that dominated the show's screen-time (that honour fell to Gabriel and Beelzebub), but in the final moments of the season there is, finally, a kiss. It is as if *Good Omens'* fandom manifested it into being, but there is no cute romcom denouement. Instead, Gaiman serves us a wonderfully complicated moment: the pair are about to be separated; Aziraphale is drunk with power and there is desperation burning on Crowley's villainous lips. Be careful what you wish for.

CHARLOTTE WILLMORE

The gaslighting, meat-cleaver-wielding villain of gory lesbian horror

There were queer whispers about *The Perfection* (2018) before it was even made. With each casting rumour, location update and boring production release, LGBTQ+ movie-gossip sites went into overdrive. Filmmaker Richard Shepard, who had already garnered a queer following directing *Girls* and *The Handmaid's Tale*, had hit on a truly enticing idea: a lesbian horror movie set in a competitive classical-music academy with *Girls* and *Get Out* star Allison Williams as its villain. Before its premier at Austin, Texas's Fantastic Fest in 2018, fans tried to predict what the movie might be about, feverishly wondering just how queer it would be. Might there be a chaste kiss, or a titillating semi-nude sex scene? Would there be romance and lesbian love? What was shown that night at Fantastic Fest, and later on Netflix, was so unexpectedly unhinged that no one knew quite where to file it. To this day, reviews for *The*

Perfection are polarized. *The New York Times* called it a 'thriller in the key of crazy'; and the squeamish few who watch it – particularly the finale scenes – might just want to try to forget it. But LGBTQ+ scream queens for whom nothing is gory enough were more than satisfied.

Williams plays Charlotte Willmore, a former cello prodigy who, on the death of her mother, decides to pick up the bow and get back into the classical-music game. Anton (Steven Weber), her manipulative former mentor, invites her to a performance in Shanghai, where she meets the charming Lizzie (Logan Browning), her replacement at Anton's creepy academy. If Charlotte seems nervous, it must be because she is meeting her rival and reconnecting with academy staff after years of musical exile. Thankfully, Charlotte and Lizzie have a connection; they go out, get riotously drunk and have incredible, passionate sex.

There is a sense of boldness here. In other works, queerness might exist only in the subtext, shown through subtle glances, or an accidental touch, but *The Perfection* makes good on its promise. These two women are attracted to one another and spend the night plucking the same string. But then, everything changes. The movie morphs alarmingly into body horror with a stack of trigger warnings: parasitic virus, self-mutilation, hallucinations, bugs, ritual sex abuse, drugging and kidnapping, ultimate revenge and so much gore. There are plot twists along the way, a revenge narrative and clunky rewinds to show different perspectives of the same scenes. At the centre of it all, wielding a meat cleaver, is Charlotte, *The Perfection*'s perfect queer villain.

As a classical-music thriller with a problematic lesbian protagonist at its heart, *Tár* it ain't. But *The Perfection* is artful in other ways. The movie is arranged in a series of movements, with Shepard as the conductor allowing himself to change the beat, the genre and even the direction of the piece. In the first movement, when Charlotte meets Lizzie in Shanghai, 'a "Black Swan" dynamic quickly begins to develop between them,' wrote Jason Bailey in *The New York Times* in 2019. 'Charlotte seems threatened but aroused by this younger prodigy. Their chemistry is electric, dramatized by a cello duet sequence that is shot and edited like a sex scene before slowly becoming one.'

In the end, yet another layer of the story is revealed and Charlotte and Lizzie work together to enact an unbelievably horrific revenge on their abusers. Production had already started on *The Perfection* when the Me Too reckoning of 2017 broke, and the movie seemed oddly prescient on its release. Viewers had read about the misogynistic monsters at large in the arts, and here, in *The Perfection*'s final movement, the abusers were finally getting their gory – but deserved – comeuppance.

Does Charlotte finally shake off her villain mantle (like she does the wig she has inexplicably been wearing throughout the movie to reveal a short, dykey hair cut)? At the end, she joins with Lizzie in another cello duet, only they now share the same instrument, and finally we see the pair as a true queer couple. They may have won against their aggressors, but have they turned into monsters themselves?

Villainous queer thanks to . . .

Jackie Bolton, Jack Bootle, Michael Chiang, Zoë Coombs-Marr, Shelly Cornick, Max Edwards, Mel Four, Scarlet Furness, Briony Gowlett, Olivia Griffiths, Willow Grogan, Cate Hall, Liz Hermann, Susanne Hillen, Jamie Holloway, Monica Hope, Kate Jinx, Joshua Mackey, Tom McDonald, Jade Moore, Jack Shoulder and Elise Solberg.